HEAVEN'S MUSCLE

HEAVEN'S MUSCLE

BREN HUGHES

Beating Heart

Hardcover ISBN: 978-0-9908908-2-9
Paperback ISBN: 978-0-9908908-1-2
Kindle ISBN: 978-0-9908908-0-5
EPUB ISBN: 978-0-9908908-3-6

Library of Congress Control Number: 2014918451

First Edition

Typesetting services by BOOKOW.COM

To Lydia,

My partner on the journey toward perfection.

"Every person must do two things alone: he must do his own believing and his own dying."

– Martin Luther

CONTENTS

Chapter Zero

Night would soon be rolling in across the junglesome mountains of Panama.

The air was humid and heavy that summer. But as the sun began to resign itself to sliding behind the mountains, a frolicsome breeze trickled upward toward the clearing where I sat alone. I was absorbing the sounds of the mountain and nurturing introspective thoughts. The year was 2000 A.D.

The mountain was called Cerro Pelado. Bald hill. About two stones' throws behind me was the schoolhouse with its thick white cinderblock walls. That's where we stayed, and where my companions were getting ready for bed. I was there in Cerro Pelado with about a dozen Americans from churches in the American southeast. It was a one-week medical mission trip.

Below my clearing was the jungle, and I could hear living things churning about in the shadowy foliage.

I imagined they were chickens and pigs. Little naked pink pigs and mangy world-weary chickens were always darting around our feet in the schoolyard, and I surmised they had ventured jungleward to seek shelter in the night.

I had been a missionary and Bible teacher. That's what I was trained to do. But on this trip I did no teaching. I was just there to be a pharmacy technician. Really what I did was put drugs in bags. My little makeshift pharmacy unit gave most of the villagers de-worming medicine and Tylenol. My job was to fill the patients' little paper bags with those two goodies plus whatever else the doctors prescribed.

That afternoon, I had joined one of the teaching teams for a trek into the village. There was a preacher and an interpreter and me and another hanger-on. I recalled stopping by the hut of the village medicine man. For a shaman he was remarkably warm and friendly, and seemed completely unperturbed by my companions' Jesus-talk. This was a man who sacrificed chickens and interpreted the will of the gods in their entrails. But I wasn't interested in changing his beliefs. Although I'd been a missionary to Russia and an associate minister in America, I was finished with converting people.

I didn't believe in the supernatural at all anymore. Why argue over religion when none of it makes any difference anyway?

In fact, I felt bad for the people I'd taught. During my college days, I'd done door-to-door evangelism campaigns in New Zealand and nine American states. I'd been reasonably effective in arranging home Bible studies and getting people to come to church. I had a teaching system that I'd inherited from my mentor. Here's what I'd teach.

We used fill-in-the-blank worksheets. The first lesson centered on sin and death, on the temptation and fall of Adam and Eve. The goal of lesson one was to stimulate guilt and a sense of lost-ness.

Lesson two was about "God's Plan." It told about God calling Abraham in the book of Genesis and God giving the Law to the Jews through Moses. The point of the lesson was to highlight the flaws in the Old Testament law.

Lesson three jumped ahead, skipping the Gospels, straight to the book of Acts. The focus was on the church, and how people in the book of Acts joined the church by being baptized. The climax of the lesson was when I asked the student whether she wanted to be baptized and join the true biblical church.

If the answer was no, I had another lesson. This lesson focused on sin and how the student was a sinner. The worksheet had two columns which contrasted heaven and hell. The point of the lesson was that the student now had the power to choose eternal torment or everlasting paradise.

And sometimes I used another worksheet. This one was about "acceptable" worship. The lesson listed five things the Bible authorizes people to do in worship: sing, pray, give, preach, and take the Lord's Supper. An accompanying diagram explained that when we add anything to these five elements ("traditions of men" like incense, praying to Mary, church raffles, taking bread but not wine for the Lord's Supper, and using musical instruments), we sin.

I'd brought some people into my church using those lessons. But that was behind me. That night in Panama, watching the sun sink below the mountains, I comforted myself with the thought that there is no God. But I still had trouble shaking the images of Jesus from the cobwebby corners of my psyche.

When I thought about the person I'd been before, I saw an image of Jesus. It's Jesus from chapter 23 of the Gospel of Matthew. That's the chapter where Jesus lets loose with a litany of "woes" or "curses" against the Pharisees, against the conservative religious establishment of his day. He told them:

Woe to you, scribes and Pharisees, hypocrites! For you make sure you give to God the correct amount of your tiniest spices – mint, dill, and cumin. But you have neglected the weightier matters of the law – justice and mercy and faith. It is these you ought to have practiced without neglecting the others. You blind guides! You strain out a gnat but swallow a camel! (NIV).

I knew that as a believer, and as a minister, I'd gotten good at straining theological gnats. Christ's "woe" always made me uncomfortable, like having itchy loose hairs inside your shirt. But another of Christ's curses against the Pharisees was even worse. That night in Cerro Pelado I could almost see Jesus superimposed against the blazing sky, his eyes fiery and angry as he pointed directly at me and shouted:

Woe to you, scribes and Pharisees, hypocrites! For you lock people out of the kingdom of heaven. You do not go in yourselves, and when others are going in, you stop them. You hypocrites cross sea and land to make a single convert, and when you do you make him twice as much a son of hell as yourselves!

I was an atheist when I went on that medical mission trip to Panama. But being an atheist was better than being a Christian Pharisee who traveled the world to make converts but who taught those converts how to be children of hell.

***

This is a book about the Holy Spirit of Jesus Christ. I know him now. This is the story of my journey from Bible-worshiper to unbeliever to partner of God. My story has helped people in the past, and I hope it will encourage you. I write this book for the glory of Jesus because I love him. And I write it for your edification because I love you, too.

I'm a believer again. And I have two battle cries. The first is from the New Testament, from Second Timothy 1:7:

God has not given us a Spirit of fear, but of power and love and self-discipline!

The second is a prayer written by W. H. H. Aitken:

Lord, take my lips and speak through them; take my mind and think through it; take my heart and set it on fire!

The Lord wanted someone to write a book for you, and using the words of young Isaiah the prophet, I said, "Here I am, Lord! Send me!" (Isaiah 6:8).

The Lord had a message for me to tell his people, and using the words of young Samuel the prophet when the Lord first called him, I said, "Speak, Lord! Your servant is listening." (1 Samuel 3:10).

One: Bad Religion

My problem in my teenage and college years was that I was into religion more than I was into Jesus. I was more interested in the Bible than in God. It's understandable, really. Religious observance and scripture were tangible and close; the Father and Son seemed far away.

That's changed now. The journey God's led me on has re-oriented my relationship to the church, the Bible, and to God. Being religious can be done wrong, and religion done wrong can be an obstacle to genuine cooperation with God.

***

To be a child in my family's house was to be at a church activity or in-between church activities. That's an exaggeration, of course, and I'm not complaining. But our calendar revolved around the three weekly worship services, youth devotionals, camps, retreats, and other assorted committees, projects, and get-togethers. My religious identity was the core aspect of myself. It was the same for my future wife. Both of us ended up majoring in religious studies at the same private Christian college.

We tried to love God, but what we'd been taught – whether intentionally or accidentally by well-meaning people – was to hype ourselves into a perpetual state of religious busy-ness. We both felt a strong sense of obligation. We had to read our Bible every day. We had to attend every worship service. We had to help the needy enough, and witness to the lost enough. To lose momentum was to be in danger of losing salvation.

I think in all honesty I was very busy with all this religious puttering about, but not always accomplishing much in terms of enlarging God's kingdom. We all loved God and the Bible, but aside from the occasional week-long mission trip to Central America, we weren't making a terribly big impact on outsiders. I knew that God had designed me to be a spiritual dynamo who changed people's lives and brought them to the Lord. But despite all my Bible knowledge and all my pew-sitting experience, I really didn't have a clear vision of what being God's ambassador looked like.

The problem was that I knew there was something I was missing. There was something else I needed to know, but I didn't know what it was. This created a percolating frustration in the back of my mind. Despite my devotion and study and religiosity I felt like a spiritual weakling.

Some people claim to be spiritual, but not religious. I think in my younger days I was religious, but not spiritual. Let's start by talking about religion.

***

I remember as a college student encountering the idea that Jesus was an enemy of religion. Some writers were fond of saying that Jesus came to destroy religion, to free people from religious obligations. I didn't understand this concept at first, but now I see that it's essentially true.

A typical definition of religion goes like this:

Religion is a set of beliefs concerning the cause, nature, and purpose of the universe, especially when considered as the creation of a superhuman agency or agencies, usually involving devotional and ritual observances, and often containing a moral code governing the conduct of human affairs. (from Dictionary.com).

That's a very broad definition, unlikely to garner much disagreement. It's got philosophy, worship, and ethics. What could be wrong with that?

But the idea of Jesus being against religion snapped into sharper focus after I read Frank Viola and George Barna's *Pagan Christianity*. Viola and Barna considered "religion" from a historical perspective and identified three key attributes that define "religion" in the traditional sense. Religion, Viola and Barna say, is a system that depends on (1) priests, (2), temples, and (3) sacrifices. This is what all pre -Christian religions had in common.

First, every religion had priests, meaning a caste of individuals distinct from the common folk who have more direct access to God. Priests serve as mediators between the people and their deity or deities.

Second, every religion has temples – holy places that are set aside for worshiping the deities. Priests and temples are tied together in that both were generally supported financially by the people.

Third, ancient religions depended on sacrifices. The oldest creation myths taught that the gods created humans because they got lazy. Mankind was created to grow crops and livestock to feed to the gods through the act of sacrifice. Ancient peoples also used sacrifices as a way of garnering benefits from the gods.

Here is how these three prongs of "religion" would interact. At the temple, priests would seek favors from the gods, and try to manipulate the gods by offering sacrifices. In this way people felt like they had gained a level of control over the world. Communities could avert disaster, they believed, if they pleased the gods. To please the gods they offered sacrifices and tried to obey the decrees handed down by the priests who spoke for the gods. It was a system of manipulation, not love. The structure emphasizes the distance, not the closeness, between the common person and the divine. Religion divided the world into sacred and profane people, sacred and profane places, sacred and profane times, and sacred and profane objects.

If we define religion through this lens, we can see, as Viola and Barna point out, that the gospel of Christ and his apostles undermined this sort of system. Christianity, in its original form, reimagined the priesthood. All followers of Christ are priests, the New Testament teaches (1 Peter 2:4-9), and Jesus is the one and only high priest (Hebrews 7:26-28). In Christ the earthly high priest (that continued to exist in Judaism) had been replaced by a heavenly one (Hebrews 8:1). But Jesus didn't eliminate the priesthood. He eliminated the "laity" and elevated all his followers to the status of sacred priests. The world of pagan nonbelievers, then, constitutes the laity to whom all Christians minister. In this way, Christ fulfilled the ancient teaching of Moses that God's people were to be a "kingdom of priests" to the pagan world. (Exodus 19:6 NIV).

The Christian movement as depicted in the New Testament also dissociated itself from physical temples. Even Judaism remained reliant on the tabernacle and then the temple. But in the teachings of Christ's apostles, the people of God are now the one true temple. The temple is a spiritual one. We who are one with Christ are the "living stones" that make up the walls of this great edifice. (1 Peter 2:5). Wherever Christians are, the temple is there. (1 Corinthians 3:16). Every place a Christian sets foot becomes a holy place because every Christian's physical body is itself a temple in miniature. (1 Corinthians 6:19). Early Christians worshiped anywhere – in homes, in catacombs, in schools – because in Christ everyone and everywhere is holy. (see John 4:21-24).

Christianity also spiritualized the concept of sacrifice. God does not need anything, the Bible teaches. And he is already willing to say yes to everything his children ask. (2 Corinthians 1:19-20; John 14:13-14). There's no need to bribe or manipulate God. Jesus demonstrated the futility of the Jewish sacrificial system. (Hebrews 10:1-14). The best sacrifice we can give God is simply to praise him and to show compassion to the poor. (Hebrews 13:15-16).

On a slightly different level, the New Testament also teaches that the Christian herself *is* the sacrifice. The only sacrifice I need to offer to God is my whole self:

I appeal to you therefore, brothers and sisters, by the mercies of God, to present your bodies as a living sacrifice, holy and acceptable to God, which is your spiritual worship. Do not be conformed to this world, but be transformed by the renewing of your minds, so that you may discern what is the will of God – what is good and acceptable and perfect. (Romans 12:1-2).

God is not interested in dead sacrifices, but living ones. In ourselves. Thus, in two ways the message of Jesus subverts the traditional concept of sacrifice. First, all that ancient sacrificial violence has been sublimated into Christ. To the extent that God may have ever wanted blood sacrifices from people, the death of Christ rendered this system obsolete. Second, the key sacrifice we need to make today is the sacrifice of our living bodies – we give ourselves wholly to God. We don't offer ourselves to placate or manipulate God. God is doing just fine, and he's already on our side. We offer our full being to the

Lord so we can to become our best, fullest, most useful selves. It's an act of aligning my will with the will of the one who designed me.

In my own personal meditation time, I sometimes imaginatively act out this passage from Romans 12. "Present your body as a living sacrifice." With these words in mind, I lie backward and offer myself to God. I envision my body on an altar. In my mind's eye I lie there with my throat exposed, willing have my body sliced open – just like the millions of animals that were sacrificed throughout the ancient world before Christ came and conquered religion. Maybe you'll want to try this exercise, too. This attitude of self-abnegation, as Paul says in Romans 12, is the heart of "spiritual worship." The result of this ego death is a recreated mind that thinks differently from how the normals think. Once the mind is freed from the world's values and paradigms, Paul suggests, the mind becomes capable of grasping God's good and perfect will.

This type of spiritual self-sacrifice is captured well in a prayer/poem by Charles de Foucauld:

My Father, I abandon myself to you. Do with me as you will.

Whatever you may do with me, I thank you.

I am prepared for anything, I accept everything.

Provided your will is fulfilled in me and in all

creatures I ask nothing more my God.

I place my soul in your hands.

I give it to you, my God,

with all the love of my heart

because I love you.

And for me it is a necessity of love,

this gift of myself,

this placing of myself in your hands

without reserve

in boundless confidence

because you are my Father.

So, having said all that, can you see how Christ was against religion? A person can follow Jesus without being overtly religious, at least in the sense I just described. The Christian is a self-contained temple, priest, and sacrifice. While Christians certainly harbor metaphysical beliefs, tell supernatural stories, and follow a moral code, they ought not be religious in the sense of relying on a human priesthood, a physical temple, or any sacrifice besides the sacrifice of one's own will to the service of God.

This is not to suggest that I should live my religion in isolation. Each of us is just a single cell in a larger organism. God's design is that we worship and rejoice and serve together in groups. But every day I meet people who feel wounded and betrayed by their churches. There are reasons why this happens so often.

***

Religion in the classical sense depends on hierarchies and boundaries. It's unavoidable. Leaders will emerge in any group. People who are trying to get things done will adopt systems and procedures and structures for making things happen. You have to draw lines once you've decided that some things are true and others are false. When a group develops a clear sense of right and wrong, there are some behaviors they can not tolerate.

So, it's natural for hierarchies and boundaries to emerge in any group of like-minded people. These hierarchies and boundaries are sources of social power. Our problem is that the Devil is highly skilled at corrupting sources of power. He can take a hierarchy or a boundary and twist it into a tool for oppressing and dividing people.

For example, leaders can be tempted into abusing their positions. And people who become invested in religion can become zealous about policing the boundaries. The Devil often tempts believers into drawing lines (around moral or doctrinal questions) where God through scripture has not drawn them. One species of this line-drawing is legalism. Legalism essentially means treating the New Testament as a rule-book. Legalists are so afraid of doing or thinking something wrong that they make new rules to shield people from breaking what they perceive to be the rules of the Bible. When a church gets carried away with legalism or an over-emphasis on authority structures, it can transmit a distorted image of God. When people are exposed to legalistic or authoritarian sermons, Bible classes, Christian schools, and sometimes family members is an image of God looming over us in the sky, shaking his finger at us and saying "No, no, no!"

Of course, the Bible's message for people outside of Christ is "repent, for the kingdom of God is at hand." (Matthew 4:17). I would never neglect the necessity of repentance. Repentance means choosing to reform your mind and recalibrate your behavior as you turn from Satan to God. Repudiating the sins in our lives is a crucial step toward becoming what God calls us to become.

But once we are in Christ, the message from God is "yes," not no. (2 Corinthians 1:19-20). "Where the Spirit of the Lord is, there is freedom." (2 Corinthians 3:17). The assembly of believers is the temple of the Holy Spirit, the Spirit of freedom. So church people should be people of freedom, people of liberation, people of "yes."

***

Consider the biblical passage that Jesus read to the people of his hometown at the beginning of his ministry:

The Spirit of the Lord is on Me,

because He has anointed Me

to preach good news to the poor.

He has sent Me

to proclaim freedom to the captives

and recovery of sight to the blind,

to set free the oppressed,

to proclaim the year of the Lord's favor.

(Luke 4:18-19, quoting Isaiah 61:1-2 NIV).

This is Christ's own manifesto. This is what he says he's all about. The message of Christ to God's children is good news and freedom. He is a liberator, not a bringer of "thou-shalt-nots." If you are poor, captive, blind, or oppressed, Christ's message for you is not a new kind of oppression but a celebration of liberation.

Now let's go a little deeper and a little weirder. The corruption, legalism, and spiritual oppression that infects so many religious communities results from an infestation of the spirit of religion.

The word "spirit" probably means one of two things to you in this context. "Spirit" can be the emotional or intellectual disposition of a person or of a group of people. This is the kind of "spirit" cheerleaders scream about when they wave their pom-poms. Or, a spirit can be an invisible personal being. I believe in the power of both types of "spirit," and that the line between the two can be fuzzy.

In the worldview of the biblical writers, the earth is haunted by malevolent spirits who specialize in emotional, physical, and spiritual bondage. I'll address this topic in detail later on. I've come to think that one of the most pernicious of these spirits is the spirit of religion. Again, think of it as a disposition if it's more comfortable for you at this point. But the spirit of religion can infiltrate a vibrant Spirit-filled Christian community and turn it into a system of religious oppression.

Once the spirit of religion settles in, a church, or aspects thereof, can degenerate into an agent for constraining and demoralizing people. Yes, lots of good stuff can still happen in religious churches, but they're never on fire like they could be. In religious churches, the teachers and leaders may manipulate people with negative emotions like fear, guilt, shame, and obligation. Religious churches become legalistic, often in subtle ways. They make conformity a test for fellowship – "believe just like me in all points or we can't worship together." These infected churches may enforce behavioral conformity, doctrinal conformity, or both. Religious churches expect people to act certain ways that go beyond what God requires in scripture. Religious churches may also discourage inquisitiveness and creativity, demanding instead that everything always be uniform and everyone always think the same thing. Again, these churches will contain many good people and will often do good things, but the religiosity in their atmosphere is putrefacient.

It reminds me of a story from my past that I'm really ashamed of.

In the summer of 1996 I was a volunteer youth ministry intern with a church in northern Virginia. We had a summer door-knocking campaign. One of the people who allowed me to do my home Bible study (with the worksheets, remember) was an elderly lady living in an apartment building. After I finished my first worksheet, the woman started telling me about her illnesses, her loneliness, her constant pain. She asked me to pray for her. I started to do it. She stopped me and asked me to put my hand on her head while I prayed.

I refused. I couldn't bring myself to do it. I don't think I'd ever seen anybody at my church put their hand on someone to pray for them. We were strictly hands-off. As much as I cared about this dear old lady, I couldn't bring myself to simply give her the gift of human touch. To lay my hands on her felt too much like something people in other churches would do – something foreign and weird and possibly unorthodox. I prayed for her. But I simply stood behind and kept my hands to myself. I could sense her disappointment. But I had to listen to my conscience.

It was so very, very wrong for me to refuse to touch that woman. Now, I put my hands on people and pray for them all the time. It's normal and natural and loving. But there had been such rigidity in my old religion, I was scared to death to do anything differently from how I'd seen it done. Lord, forgive me! I was in captivity to the spirit of religion, and had not yet been set free by God's Spirit of freedom.

Using obligation, shame, and guilt in an attempt to modify people's behavior is not what freedom looks like. That is not the recipe for joy. It's not biblical. It's not the sort of environment where the Spirit of God can do its best work. Behavioral constraints based on negative emotions come not from God, but from the Devil. And Jesus very specifically wants to free you from them. In fact, he has called me to help free his people from the spirit of religion so they can know the Spirit of the Lord, and that "where the Spirit of the Lord is, there is freedom." (2 Corinthians 3:17).

God's children should not be beaten into submission with guilt, shame, and obligation. Instead, God's children make the choice to mold their characters to the character of Christ for positive reasons – because they love him and enjoy making him happy.

***

My wife and I love to serve each other. But I don't do it because I'm afraid of what will happen if my wife is displeased. I am invested in her happiness because I feel such gratitude and honor that she chose me. It's the same way with my service to God.

***

Here is a short, non-exhaustive list of features that differentiate good religion from bad religion. Jesus said people and churches will be judged by their fruits, meaning the effects they have on the world. (Matthew 7:19-21; John 15:1-2; Revelation 2:1-5; see also Luke 3:7-14). The first crucial fruit is that the followers of Jesus are known by their love. (John 13:35). So, a good church is one that loves like Jesus – with compassion and self-sacrifice. Love is not sentimentality. Love seeks the best in others and cares about integrity and truth. (John 14:15). In following Jesus's example, the church will be especially loving toward outsiders and the poor and disadvantaged.

It makes me think of what James the Lord's brother said – that God's definition of religion is "to care for orphans and widows in their distress, and to keep oneself unstained by the world." (James 1:27). And it reminds me of Christ's parable of the sheep and the goats from Matthew 25, where the thing that separates the saved from the lost on the day of judgment is whether people fed the hungry, clothed the naked, and visited sick people and prisoners.

Second, good religion produces people with integrity and high moral character. That's because every Christian is someone who's in the process of repentance. The biblical word for repentance – *metanoia* – contains the Greek word for the intellect coupled with a word that signals an alternative pathway. Repentance means adopting an alternative frame of reference from the world around us. It means buying into a new worldview. This alternative worldview in turn affects our values, which affects our behavior. (See Acts 2:19-20). Repentance thus comes from the inside out. Because Christians, as citizens of a spiritual kingdom, think differently from people living in Satan's kingdom, they necessarily act differently. Their ethics are unimpeachable.

Third, there are also doctrinal teachings that are crucial to the health of a church. The letter of First John, for example, teaches that denying that Jesus was fully human or that Jesus was the Jewish Messiah is fatal to a person's faith. (1 John 2:22; 4:1-3). A good church has good biblical teaching. Putting these first three points together, we can say that a good church displays biblical truth and sacrificial love in a way that brings people to repentance. (1 Corinthians 14:24-26).

Another way of approaching this list is to note that good churches will center their worship on the triune God and expend their energy in healing the world God loves so much. Christians delight in praising their Father, in following the teaching and example of Jesus, and experiences the comforting and empowering presence of the Spirit. Good churches do not revolve around the church leadership. The church itself does not take center stage in the place of Christ. Good churches don't try to control people through obligation, guilt, shame, or threats. They admit their sins. They are safe places where abuse is never tolerated.

The thing that most attracts me to a church is a palpable sense that the Spirit is present among the people and is actively leading them. When I get in a group like that, the Spirit becomes contagious. Lives get radically changed on a regular basis. People pray for each other at the drop of the hat. When churches like that worship, the people reek of joy and get carried away in the pleasure of praise.

***

It's the presence of the Holy Spirit that enables me to be heaven's muscle on earth. When I allow my mind to be synchronized with the mind of Christ, I become empowered to do things I could not otherwise imagine.

This is a story about my friend Jon. Jon and I grew up in the same denomination. He's younger than me, but he attended one of the same universities I attended. This story happened while he was an undergraduate student. Jon and I only met this year. I invited him to our house one day after church, and he told us this story.

It was the morning of September 11, 2001. The day of the terrorist attack. Like many Americans that day, my friend Jon was watching his television in horror. But the thing about Jon that's different from me was that as a college student Jon was already hearing the voice of God. As he watched New York burn, Jon felt he was getting transmissions from heaven. Something in his gut told him he needed to go to New York City.

Then Jon got a call from one of his friends. "Are you feeling what I'm feeling," the friend asked. He was getting the signals too. Two other friends also called. All four young men had a burning sensation in their hearts telling them to head to New York immediately. So they packed up Jon's car and took off from Nashville.

The thing about 9/11 was that everybody was expecting another attack. The National Guard swooped in and shut down New York City. The Guard and the police blocked the bridges and tunnels. NYC was on lockdown. Every airplane in the country was grounded. Jon and his friends knew God wanted them to go toward ground zero. But getting there looked impossible. They went anyway.

Jon had a friend who was on the ministry staff at a church in Manhattan. Jon phoned this friend as he drove and told him he and three buddies were coming to New York to help. The minister friend appreciated the gesture, but doubted they'd be allowed anywhere near Manhattan.

At last, the guys arrived at the bridge that would carry them from New Jersey to Manhattan. Their hearts sank as they saw that the bridge was blocked by police cars and National Guard vehicles. There were even two tanks posted at the bridge entrance, their guns pointed right into oncoming traffic. The uniformed men with guns sent a clear message: You shall not pass.

Jon drove his vehicle to the barricade and stopped. He wondered whether this was the end of the line. But then a National Guardsman motioned with his hand, and officers removed the barricades. Even one of the tanks moved aside so Jon's car could pass. Without a word, the Guardsman waved Jon and his friends onto the bridge.

The young men screamed in disbelief as they drove across the deserted bridge onto Manhattan Island. What in the world just happened?

Jon phoned his minister friend again. The guys from Nashville would see him shortly.

When they arrived at the church building, Jon and his friends loaded Jon's car with supplies for ground zero. The minister instructed him to take the supplies to a particular dock where they could load the supplies on a boat. Jon complied.

But when Jon and friends arrived at the dock, a worker told them the boat was full; they'd just missed it. He suggested they try the next dock. At the next dock down, it was the same story. They went to a third dock, and again they were told the boat was full. The group ran out of docks. There was nothing left to do but drive straight to the World Trade Center – right into ground zero itself.

On the way, a police car started following Jon, its lights flashing. Was this the end of the road? Jon kept driving slowly, but the officer never motioned for them to pull over. Soon two other police cars flanked Jon's car. He was being given a police escort. This was a good thing, because there were snipers all over the city who probably had their rifle scopes trained on Jon's car. Finally, Jon's crew arrived at ground zero. The police cars pulled away. In his rearview mirror, Jon could see them going back the direction they came.

***

The scene at ground zero was eerie and disquieting. The air was heavy with dust and smoke. Firemen trudged around coated in white powder like shell-shocked ghosts.

There was a tent where aid workers were handling emergency supplies for the people at ground zero, who were mostly first responders and families of victims. But there was nowhere for Jon to park. Suddenly, an ambulance fired up its siren and pulled away. A survivor had been found somewhere. And a parking spot was suddenly open for Jon's vehicle. He pulled up right against the fence surrounding the disaster zone.

Jon and his friends unloaded their supplies and spent a few hours among the firemen who came by the tent. They listened to the firemen's stories and prayed with them in the Spirit. Many of the firemen had lost friends in the building collapse. Many of them felt survivor's guilt for escaping alive. Jon and his friends gave them their sympathy and words of hope.

Then a group of Franciscan monks walked by. They asked the Nashville lads whether they'd like to join them. The group traveled by foot to a location where bodies were being housed. It was a store. The merchandise was gone from the shelves and in its place were bodies and body parts. This was where rescue workers brought the families of victims to see if they could identify bodies. It was a place of death and trauma. Again, Jon and his friends were able to love and minister to people. They prayed with those who grieved. It was exhausting, but rewarding. At the end of the day, the young men returned to the tent.

Waiting for them at the tent was a reporter from a prominent Manhattan radio station. She asked Jon for a live interview. Jon was able to tell New York City the story about how God had sent him on a mission from Nashville, about how God made it possible for them to penetrate the city despite the lockdown, and about how the Lord had brought them straight to the heart of grief, into the holy moment of awe and terror that greeted the first responders and bereaved families at the site of the attack. Not only was Jon able to minister, he was then able to bear witness to the Lord's work to an audience that potentially numbered in the millions.

Jon is now an associate pastor at the church where I worship in Kentucky. He has a beautiful family, and everywhere he goes he blesses and enriches people. I am thrilled to be his friend.

I want to be used by God like he used Jon and his friends on 9/11. I want to have the guts to go to strange and dangerous places, knowing that when the Lord calls me there he'll take care of me. And in following God's voice, I'd like to see unexplainable things – the sort of things that happened to people in the Bible.

***

Jon's story illustrates the kind of Spirit-led lifestyle I'm advocating. It's fundamentally different from the way I used to try to experience God.

I once adhered to a false religion. I call it bibliolatry. That's "Bible" plus "idolatry," from the Greek *latreuo*, meaning "I worship." I'm talking about worshiping the Bible.

Again, I'm not blaming my parents or the church I grew up in. I'm not throwing anybody under the bus aside from my old self and the Devil.

One of the Devil's tricks is to get people who think they're Christians to pour their attention and adoration and energy into something that isn't God, but is kind of close to God. Some people do this with political and social causes. Some people do it with their families or friends. Others become devoted to defending their favorite theological system. I watch so many Christian writers on the internet who spend their days arguing over pet doctrines and interpretations. Yes, God's truth must be defended, but when a writer is always hammering a specific doctrine one could be forgiven for concluding that the writer has started worshiping and serving the belief system itself.

I think I knew in the back of my mind, growing up in the church environment that I did, that I was at risk of worshiping the Bible rather than Jesus. Many members of my natal church (by natal, I mean the church I grew up in) did not believe that God worked directly in the world today apart from invisible nudges called providence. We did not believe that God would personally guide, teach, or empower us. We would have interpreted Jon's 9/11 story as nothing more than a series of odd coincidences. To us, the Bible was our only source of information about God. Spirituality meant following the Bible as closely as possible – both in your lifestyle and in your doctrinal beliefs. There was little tolerance for doctrinal error because we believed the Bible was unified and clear.

Because the Bible, to us, was the only way to hear God's voice, we tended to fuss over it quite a bit. I personally was obsessed with knowing everything about it. It hurt my heart that some passages in the Bible were difficult to understand. As a young adult, I was determined to learn the biblical languages because I thought that in doing so I could uncover the one true meaning to every verse in the Bible. To me, knowing the Bible was the key to salvation.

Of course, this was wrong. The Bible doesn't save people. God does it in Christ. I was like the people Christ addressed in John 5:39-40: "You search the scriptures because you think that in them you have eternal life; and it is they that testify on my behalf. Yet you refuse to come to *me* and have life." God doesn't expect us to understand everything the prophets ever wrote. In fact, the prophets themselves sometimes didn't understand their own messages. (1 Peter 1:10-12). My salvation does not depend on my intellectual knowledge of the contents of the Bible,

33

but on my existential knowledge of the person of Jesus Christ.

Anyway, because of my religious heritage and my general intellectual proclivities, I was highly at risk for becoming a bibliolater. I think God did something to try to divert me from that misbegotten path.

***

It was the summer after my freshman year at college. I was taking a short course on the Gospel of John, and for each class session we were assigned certain passages to memorize. I was alone in my dorm room one evening, memorizing a passage from John chapter six. My Bible was spread open on my bed and I paced the floor in our little wood-paneled room, repeating the passage so it would be ingrained on my brain.

John six is the chapter where Jesus feeds the multitude with five loaves and two fish. The crowd picks up on the similarity between this miracle and the miracle of manna with Moses in the wilderness. Jesus uses the bread and fish to make the point that becoming spiritually united to him is the key to obtaining freedom and wholeness. Jesus says,

I am the bread of life. The one who comes to me shall never hunger, and the one who believes in me shall never thirst. (John 6:35).

As I said this line aloud, something about it hooked me. I felt driven to say it over and over again. I kept pacing back and forth across the room, repeating:

I am the bread of life. The one who comes to me shall never hunger, and the one who believes in me shall never thirst.

I am the bread of life. The one who comes to me shall never hunger, and the one who believes in me shall never thirst.

I am the bread of life. He who comes to me shall never hunger, and he who believes in me shall never thirst.

At that moment, I intuitively comprehended the power of that scripture in ways I'd never be able to express. It was moving me. It was becoming a mantra. I felt that Christ and I were drawing closer and closer with each utterance. Never hunger, never thirst. I had been so hungry for the Lord, so hungry for love, so thirsty for answers. A light was shining through the cracks in my mind.

And then it hit me. Literally. Whump! It felt like something invisible *punched me in the chest.* I fell backward onto my bed with a heavy thump. In an instant, I was lying on my back with the wind knocked out of me. I just lay there for a while, startled, my eyes wide, struggling to regain my breath. I was in shock. Something strange and supernatural had just happened to me.

I did not believe an experience like that was possible. But there it was. *Somebody* knocked the wind out of me.

In the ensuing months, I kept that passage in John close to my heart. After my experience I tried several times to preach from that passage and convey the power and beauty of it. But I always ended up frustrated. I was never able to recapture that feeling and translate it into words. That passage had hit me in the heart, but I lacked the communicative talent to convey the same effect to others.

The way I've interpreted that unusual event is that God was trying to drive home the point that it was *Jesus himself* who could fulfill my spiritual longings. He knew I was on the path to bibliolatry. Socking me in the chest while I was fixating on John 6:35 was his way of telling me to keep my eyes on Jesus. Focus on the Son, he was saying, and don't get lost in the endless wars over words and translations and doctrines. My salvation from frustration would not come from the text or from the church. It could only be found in the living person of Jesus Christ. The one who comes to *him* shall never hunger, and the one who trusts in *him* will never thirst.

For a while after that experience I lived on a spiritual high. I felt Christ was close at hand, walking beside me as I drank in the beauty of the trees and the sunshine and the sounds around campus. I felt he was real, and that he was my companion and friend.

But those feelings faded. I delved deeper and deeper into Greek. I became fixated on translation philosophies and textual criticism. The religio-academic environment of the university kept my attention focused on doctrinal issues and theological minutia. God taught me a lesson, and gave me a feeling. But the feeling slipped away and I forgot the lesson. By the time I'd finished my bachelor's and master's degrees, God felt far away again. Even studying the Bible brought me no comfort anymore. When I tried to read scripture, my mind would do everything but allow the text to speak to me with a living voice. I would automatically back-translate everything I read, or else think about how each scripture I encountered related to different doctrinal arguments. In my hands, the Bible felt like a cadaver on a dissection table, not a "living and active" spiritual organism.

I had fallen into worshiping an idol, a man-made object, rather than the God that the object was meant to glorify. My theological education had birthed my spiritual nadir.

A few months after I graduated with a master's degree in New Testament studies and biblical languages, I no longer believed in God at all. For almost three years I remained an unbeliever. My training in ministry seemed to have been for naught.

But I was not truly lost. I still had love in my heart. I was still on a quest for truth. God was actually leading me on a journey that would take me places I could never imagine. But he had to break my intellect first. He had to sandblast away the chains that the spirit of religion and legalism and bibliolatry had wrapped around me. My loss of faith would ultimately prove to be a step toward freedom.

Two: God's Plan to Unshackle Humanity

The story of the New Testament is the story of God through Jesus in the Spirit bringing people from darkness into light. Your journey will be different from mine. But God leads us all on a mission. Recall again Jesus's personal mission statement from Luke 4:18-19:

The Spirit of the Lord is on me,

because he has anointed me

to proclaim good news to the poor.

He has sent me to proclaim freedom for the prisoners

and recovery of sight for the blind,

to set the oppressed free,

to proclaim the year of the Lord's favor. (NIV)

As we walk this dusty planet, we become captured by bad ideas, bad relationships, bad habits. And sin. But Christ calls us to follow him out of these dungeons. And in turn, he calls us to free others.

One passage that beautifully captures the way the Spirit of Christ brings vision and liberation is found in what we know as Paul's letter to the Ephesians. Here is the "before" half of Paul's "before-and-after" description of humanity (and individuals) in need of Jesus:

You were dead through the trespasses and sins in which you once lived, following the course of this world, following the ruler of the power of the air, the spirit that is now at work among those who are disobedient. All of us once lived among them in the passions of our flesh, following the desires of flesh and senses, and we were by nature children of wrath, like everyone else. (Ephesians 2:1-3).

What is the state of fallen human beings who live under the curse and outside the blessings of Christ? Such people have a deadness inside. They live in sin, which literally means they miss the targets they're aiming at. They're being swept downstream in the river of the world's ways. They may think they're in control – that they're piloting their own lives – but they aren't. They live under the influence of evil spirits. The "ruler of the power of the air" is of course Satan, and he's "at work" among the lost, feeding them lies like he always does. How do folks live when they're under demonic control? They live like animals, doing whatever their bodies tell them to do. While they may not appear miserable, their state is essentially a state of "wrath" when compared to the freedom they could otherwise enjoy.

Check out what happens when God enters the picture. Paul continues:

But God, who is rich in mercy, out of the great love with which he loved us even when we were dead through our trespasses, made us alive together with Christ – by grace you have been saved – and raised us up with him and seated us with him in the heavenly places in Christ Jesus, so that in the ages to come he might show the immeasurable riches of his grace in kindness toward us in Christ Jesus. For by grace you have been saved through faith, and this is not your own doing; it is the gift of God – not the result of works, so that no one may boast. For we are what he has made us, created in Christ Jesus for good works, which God prepared beforehand to be our way of life. (Ephesians 2:4-9).

Notice here God's power to lift people out of the darkest places in life and make them shine. It's one of his favorite tricks. Here, Paul calls it a resurrection and enthronement.

***

Let me be honest and say that when I became an atheist, I felt incredibly relieved. Ditching religion was like taking a huge weight off my back. There was so much condemnation and guilt and paranoia in the church that I didn't have to deal with anymore. It was actually a happy time.

I realize my case is kind of unusual. I have other friends who lost their faith and for them it was a terrible grieving process. But for me, it was instant relief. By shucking off religion, including my religion's concept of God as a kind of angry dad with lots of nitpicky rules, I actually took a step closer to the true God. Again, I'm not saying that the people in my church were bad and that everything was terrible. But facets of the denomination of my youth, as a vulnerable human institution, had been infiltrated and infected by the "ruler of the power of the air" and his Pharisaical spirit of religion.

But let me step away from my personal story for a bit. I want to focus on Jesus. I haven't said nearly enough about him yet. If Jesus came, as some scholars say, to free people from religion, then what was his strategy? Here's a quick sketch.

***

First, at the age of 30, Jesus was baptized by his cousin, the prophet John. As a result of being baptized in harmony with God's plan, Jesus received the Holy Spirit. This gift of the Holy Spirit came with an "anointing," a sense of purpose or of having a mission that God had equipped him to accomplish. To begin this mission, Jesus prepared himself by abandoning society for 40 days to meditate in isolation – to speak to and listen to God. However, this time was also a period of testing, as the Devil appeared and put Jesus's integrity to the test through a series of increasingly despicable temptations.

Having proved his mettle, and having prepared himself through prayer and fasting, Jesus emerged onto the scene fully formed, casting out demons, healing the sick, and preaching that prophecies were being fulfilled in him. Also from the beginning, Jesus began assembling a team of disciples whom he trained to do the same things he did – to pray, to heal, to preach, to battle dark spirits. Jesus gave them spiritual "authority" to do all these things, and promised that in the future they would also receive the same Spirit that energized him. Thus, carrying the same power source as Christ himself, his followers – all of them, not just the original twelve – could then go transform their world. The spirit of religion and the spirit of lies and the spirit of sin would flee in the presence of the spiritual power that the Jesus people would carry with them. That's the general outline of what happens in the four gospels.

And it worked. Initially, Jesus failed to win the hearts of many people. And so did his followers. But within a few years, both Jews and pagans were flooding into Rabbi Jesus's messianic movement. Over the next three hundred years, the majority of the Roman Empire would become at least nominally Christian.

How did this phenomenal growth happen? The historian Ramsay McMullen sought to answer this question in his book, *Christianizing the Roman Empire*. McMullen studied written sources from the first four centuries A.D. that describe why certain groups of people adopted Christianity. Almost invariably, McMullen found, the conversions resulted from the Jesus people performing signs and wonders that proved the Christian God was the true God. In this way, the Lord's Spirit-filled people had changed the world forever.

***

But now let's slow down a bit. While we're thinking about Jesus, let's explore a little theology – Christology to be specific. Although we could spend the rest of this book examining Christ's teachings or interpreting his mighty acts, it's also useful to think about Christ's identity philosophically. The theological aspects of the Jesus story – including the meaning of his incarnation, atoning death, and resurrection – are important facets of God's plan to unshackle humanity. Because it's Christ through his Spirit who breaks our spiritual and emotional chains.

There are various modes in which people can talk philosophically about Jesus, and they all contribute to a holistic and robust understanding of the Savior. As mainstream Christianity has always affirmed, Jesus of Nazareth was both fully human and fully divine. And this is a mystery and paradox that defies clear explanation. Thus, at times a person might focus on "high Christology," which emphasizes Christ's divinity. Colossians 1:13-20 is a great example of "high Christology." The same goes for Titus 2:13 and Second Peter 1:1, both of which refer to Jesus Christ as our "God and Savior."

At other times, a person might prefer to focus on "low Christology," which emphasizes Christ's humanness. "Low Christology" reminds us of our connection and similarity to Jesus, and how he understands us because he lived a fully human life. (Hebrews 2:17).

I most often find myself focusing on "kenotic Christology," which emphasizes the incarnation. "Kenotic" is from the Greek word *kenosis*, which means "pouring out" or "emptying." Paul uses the verb form of this word in Philippians 2, where he describes the true impact of the Son of God becoming a human being:

though he was in the form of God, [Christ] did not regard equality with God as something to be exploited,

but emptied himself,

taking the form of a slave,

being born in human likeness.

And being found in human form,

he humbled himself

and became obedient to the point of death – even death on a cross.

Although the pre-incarnate Christ shared in God's form (*morphe*, or essential qualities), he willingly "emptied himself" (that's *kenosis*) of his divine attributes in order to become fully human for the purpose of human salvation. But he not only lowered himself to becoming human, he lived a slave-like life in his utter and absolute obedience to his Father's will. What an incredible gift, and at what incredible expense! The power and extravagance of Christ's altruism can leave a person breathless. But Paul continues the story, and explains what happened as a result of Christ's voluntary diminution:

Therefore God also highly exalted him

and gave him the name that is above every name,

so that at the name of Jesus every knee should bend,

in heaven and on earth and under the earth,

and every tongue should confess that Jesus Christ is Lord,

to the glory of God the Father.

Thus, the story of Christ's work in this passage both begins and ends with high Christology. Because he radically lowered himself, Jesus is even more worthy of all praise and worship than he was when he existed in the "form" of God before the incarnation. It's an incredible narrative that rewards careful study.

It is also worth noting that Paul's description of Christ's *kenosis* in Philippians is presented in the context of encouraging believers to imitate Christ's self-abnegation. The survival of the church, Paul says, depends on each of us being willing to empty ourselves. But if we do humble ourselves, the text implies, God will also exalt us in the end.

But all this philosophical metaphysical stuff is only part of the full Jesus package. The things Christ taught, for example, are absolutely critical. But what I want to focus on in this chapter is the overarching narrative of his deeds, and how he instructed his followers to recapitulate everything he did.

***

In the Gospels of Matthew and Luke, we first encounter Jesus as a tiny embryo in a teenage girl's womb. Soon, the Lord appears as a baby. A wet, floppy baby just like every other human baby, crying, pooping, struggling to move his head. In Luke we see him briefly as a tweenager, showing a bit of precocity in his theological inquisitiveness, but also something of a troublemaker. Luke's story has Jesus blithely discussing scripture with a bunch of experts in the temple complex while his family frantically searches Jerusalem trying to find him.

How would this young man go about the business of saving the world? I am not thinking about the atonement of the cross and the resurrection at this point. Instead, I want to ask: now that God walks among men in fully human form, how will this God-man go about his task of rejuvenating hearts and disseminating his message that salvation has come?

Before the Gospels depict Jesus working a single miracle or preaching a single sermon, all four books introduce the reader to Jesus's cousin John. John lives in the wilderness, eating bugs, dressing like a cave-man, and shouting at people to repent. John was odd, but many people understood that John was the first bona fide firing-on-all-cylinders prophet that the Jews had seen in generations. Scandalously, he told the Jews they needed to ceremonially bathe themselves ("be baptized") in order to have their sins forgiven, as if they were unclean Gentiles and not God's chosen people.

It is into this fascinating milieu that Jesus steps. Jesus himself trudges into the wilderness and asks John to baptize him. John balks. He knows Jesus is even more special than himself. But Jesus insists that being baptized is the right thing to do, so John acquiesces.

Jesus's baptism in the Jordan River at about age 30 becomes a major turning point in his life. When it happens, God speaks. A voice from the sky proclaims "This is my beloved son." A dove flies down and lands on Jesus. Perhaps most important of all, this dove is the Holy Spirit, which now fills Jesus and supercharges him with courage and power. Until this point, the Gospels have not shown Jesus working wonders or preaching. He is but a man, the son of a carpenter. But now things will be different.

Having been filled with the Spirit and then spiritually sharpened through 40 days of testing, Jesus explodes onto the Galilean scene, healing the sick, doing battle with demons, and preaching a variation on John's message to "repent, for the kingdom of God is at hand." You can read about these early experiences of Jesus in Matthew 3-4; Mark 1, Luke 3-4; and John 1.

***

I want to emphasize at this point something I used to misunderstand. I grew up imagining that Jesus healed people and cast out demons under his own power, and that he raised himself from the dead by his own inherent power. But the biblical authors state quite plainly that this was not the case. Instead, all of Christ's miracles were done by the power of the Holy Spirit. And it was the Holy Spirit that raised Jesus's body from the dead, not Jesus's own Spirit. This is a crucial teaching because the Holy Spirit, the same power that worked in Christ, lives and works in all God's people. Jesus himself makes this clear, and carefully explains that his followers will have access to the same miraculous gifts, the same supernatural courage, the same divine wisdom and knowledge, that Jesus experienced.

Let me show you. Right after Jesus's baptism, after the Holy Spirit of God has descended on him "in bodily form like a dove," Jesus is then described as "full of the Holy Spirit" (Luke 4:1). Then the Spirit "leads" or "sends" Jesus into the wilderness, where he fasts and faces temptation. After his sojourn in the wilderness, Jesus returns to Galilee "in the power of the Spirit" and begins his ministry (Luke 4:14). When Jesus preaches his first sermon in his hometown, he begins by quoting the book of the prophet Isaiah. "The Spirit of the Lord is on me, and has anointed me" with a mission, he announces. (Luke 4:18). In Luke 10:21, Jesus says a prayer of thanksgiving while "full of joy through the Holy Spirit." The link here is clear between Christ's reception of the Spirit and his subsequent divinely-guided actions and words.

In Matthew 12, Jesus again quotes Isaiah and applies the prophet's words to himself:

Here is my servant, whom I have chosen,

my beloved, with whom my soul is well pleased.

I will put my Spirit upon him,

and he will proclaim justice to the Gentiles.

(Matthew 12:18, quoting Isaiah 42:1).

In this same chapter, Jesus explains that he casts out demons "by the Spirit of God." (Matthew 12:28).

In Acts 1, Jesus is said to have instructed his disciples "through the Holy Spirit." (Acts 1:2). Later in Acts, the apostle Peter tells the first Gentile convert Cornelius the message about Jesus. He tells Cornelius that he has already heard "how God anointed Jesus of Nazareth with the Holy Spirit and with power; how he went about doing good and healing all who were oppressed by the devil, for God was with him." (Acts 10:38). The formula here is that Jesus was anointed by God with the Holy Spirit and power, and that this man Jesus was then able to heal people, to speak God's truth, and overpower the Devil because "God was with him."

The resurrection of Christ was also something the Holy Spirit did. Peter writes that "Christ was . . . put to death in the body but *made alive* by the Spirit, through whom also he went and preached to the spirits in prison. . . ." (1 Peter 3:18-19). Paul writes, "If the Spirit of him who raised Jesus from the dead dwells in you, he who raised Christ from the dead will give life to your mortal bodies also through his Spirit that dwells in you." (Romans 8:11).

Nowhere in the New Testament is Jesus described as doing supernatural things by virtue of his own inherent power. Remember from Philippians 2 that he "emptied himself" of those things when he decided to become a human infant.

My point is that the New Testament teaches that all the cool and miraculous and wise things Jesus did and said were actually done by the power of the Spirit, which anointed and filled him. Jesus was a man, but he was a man filled with the Spirit "without measure" or "without limit." (John 3:34).

That explains why Jesus could so matter-of-factly tell his disciples that they would be able to do everything he did, and even more! Check out this conversation between Phillip and Jesus in John 14:

Philip said to him, "Lord, show us the Father, and we will be satisfied." Jesus said to him, "Have I been with you all this time, Philip, and you still do not know me? Whoever has seen me has seen the Father. How can you say, 'Show us the Father'? Do you not believe that I am in the Father and the Father is in me?

The words that I say to you I do not speak on my own; but the Father who dwells in me does his works. Believe me that I am in the Father and the Father is in me; but if you do not, then believe me because of the works themselves. Very truly, I tell you, the one who believes in me will also do the works that I do and, in fact, will do greater works than these, because I am going to the Father. I will do whatever you ask in my name, so that the Father may be glorified in the Son. If in my name you ask me for anything, I will do it. (John 14:8-14).

Jesus goes on to explain in this chapter that after he is gone, his followers will receive the Holy Spirit, which will in turn teach them "everything" and remind them of what Jesus taught. (John 14:26). The Spirit, he says, would guide them into "all truth." (John 16:13). Jesus gives a similar teaching in Mark 16:17-18:

And these signs will accompany those who believe: In my name they will drive out demons; they will speak in new languages; they will pick up snakes; if they should drink anything deadly, it will never harm them; they will lay hands on the sick, and they will get well.

It is important to note that Jesus does not confine these miraculous powers solely to the twelve apostles. He says the miracles "will accompany those who believe." He says "the one who believes in me" will do the same works he did, and even greater ones. The implication is that if I am a believer (one who trusts

Jesus and becomes dependable), then these signs and wonders are available to me!

***

The rest of the New Testament confirms that this supernatural knowledge and gifting was ubiquitous among followers of Christ.

Before Christ ascended to heaven, he told his disciples, speaking of the Spirit, "I am going to send you what my Father has promised; but stay in [Jerusalem] until you have been clothed with power from on high." (Luke 24:49). When Luke continues his narrative in the book of Acts, he elaborates on Christ's final words:

Do not leave Jerusalem, but wait for the gift my Father promised, which you have heard me speak about. For John baptized with water, but in a few days you will be baptized with the Holy Spirit. . . . But you will receive power when the Holy Spirit comes on you; and you will be my witnesses in Jerusalem, and in all Judea and Samaria, and to the ends of the earth. (Acts 1:4-5, 8).

And it happened just as Jesus predicted.

In Acts chapter 2, a sound like a violent wind disrupts central Jerusalem and tongues of fire appear on the heads of the 12 apostles (or more likely the gender-mixed group of 120 disciples). The fire indicates that these people are now "filled with the Holy Spirit." They start "to speak in tongues as the Spirit enabled them." After a curious crowd gathers at the scene, Peter informs the onlookers that this experience is what the prophet Joel had foretold:

In the last days, God says, I will pour out my Spirit on all people. Your sons and your daughters will prophesy, your young men will see visions, your old men will dream dreams. Even on my servants, both men and women, I will pour out my Spirit in those days, and they will prophesy. (Acts 2: 17-18, quoting Joel 2:28-29).

Peter then explains to the crowd that Jesus was raised from the dead, and "Exalted to the right hand of God, he has received from the Father the promised Holy Spirit and has poured out what you now see and hear." Again, notice the link between the reception of the Spirit, the gift of supernatural power, and the ability to witness on behalf of Jesus.

When the crowd feels moved to respond to Peter's sermon, Peter tells them to

Repent and be baptized, every one of you, in the name of Jesus Christ for the forgiveness of your sins. And you will receive the gift of the Holy Spirit. The promise is for

you and your children and for all who are far off – for all whom the Lord our God will call. (Acts 2:38- 39).

What had the apostles received that enabled them to speak in other languages and to preach boldly the whole truth about Christ? It was the Holy Spirit. And Peter promised that this same gift of the Spirit would be given to those who responded to his sermon. And to their children. And the gift was "for all who are far away," for everyone the Lord would call. That sounds pretty universal to me.

Let me pause here for just a moment and say something about baptism. The word "baptize" is actually just a Greek word in English letters. It's the word ancient Greek speakers like the New Testament authors used to describe a dipping or immersion in water. The prophet John associated it with repentance and forgiveness of sins. (Luke 3:3). Jesus did it to be fully righteous. (Matthew 3:13-17). And Peter here on the Day of Pentecost in Acts 2 told the people in Jerusalem to do it for the forgiveness of sins, and that they'd then receive the gift of the Holy Spirit. In the New Testament, the act of baptism is associated with getting "into Christ." (Romans 6:3; Galatians 3:27). You might think of it as being like a dedication ceremony to Jesus – almost like a marriage. Because baptism is associated with the forgiveness of sins (Luke 3:3; Acts 2:38; 1 Peter 3:21) and with receiving the Spirit (1 Corinthians 12:13), I wonder whether a failure to be baptized might be a hindrance to becoming empowered by the Spirit. I am aware that Cornelius received the Spirit before his baptism (Acts 10:44-48), but I think the text implies that this deviation from the norm was important to convince Peter that Gentiles could be Christians. God is not limited by formulas. But the Gospels and Acts suggest that baptism is pretty important. If you haven't yet been baptized like Jesus and the people in Acts chapter two were baptized, I encourage you to do it as soon as possible.

Now, back to our story about the history of spiritual empowerment in the New Testament.

***

So far, I am not seeing anything in the relevant passages that would limit the miraculous indwelling of the Spirit to a limited group of believers. Jesus and Peter seem to clearly think the gifts of the Spirit are for everyone and bear no expiration date.

Consider this story from Acts 4. The Jewish leaders order that Peter be arrested. Peter speaks to these leaders the morning after his imprisonment. In verse 8 Peter is said to be "filled with the Holy Spirit" as he speaks. The rulers and teachers are amazed by the way he talks to them, and they end up releasing him. When Peter returns to the other believers, the whole group prays, and then "the place where they were meeting was shaken. And *they were all filled with the Holy Spirit and spoke the word of God boldly.*" (Acts 4:31).

In the next chapter, Peter is again summoned before the authorities. Peter and his friends explain that they were "witnesses" of Christ's resurrection and ascension, "and so is the Holy Spirit, whom God has given to those who obey him." (Acts 5:32). Here again, the Spirit is described as a gift God gives to those who obey.

Near the end of the first century, the apostle John wrote to a group of Christians and reminded them, "you have been anointed by the Holy One, and all of you have knowledge . . . . The anointing you received from Him remains in you, and you don't need anyone to teach you. Instead, His anointing teaches you about all things and is true." (1 John 2:20, 27).

Paul also described this indwelling, gift, or anointing of the Spirit as a universal Christian experience. He tells the Christians at Rome that the "just requirement" of God's law is "fulfilled in us, who walk not according to the flesh but according to the Spirit." He explains:

[Y]ou are not in the flesh; you are in the Spirit, since the Spirit of God dwells in you. Anyone who does not have the Spirit of Christ does not belong to him. But if Christ is in you, though the body is dead because of sin, the Spirit is life because of righteousness. If the Spirit of him who raised Jesus from the dead dwells in you, he who raised Christ from the dead will give life to your mortal bodies also through his Spirit that dwells in you. (Romans 8:4 -11).

Paul tells the Roman Christians that "by the Spirit" they can "put to death" their destructive behaviors. He continues:

For all who are led by the Spirit of God are children of God. For you did not receive a spirit of slavery to fall back into fear, but you have received a spirit of adoption. When we cry, "Abba! Father!" it is that very Spirit bearing witness with our spirit that we are children of God, and if children, then heirs, heirs of God and joint heirs with Christ. (Romans 8:13-17).

"Likewise," Paul says, "the Spirit helps us in our weakness; for we do not know how to pray as we ought, but that very Spirit intercedes with sighs too deep for words. And God, who searches the heart, knows what is the mind of the Spirit, because the Spirit intercedes for the saints according to the will of God." (Romans 8:26-27).

The New Testament is saturated with this language about Christians being given, led by, taught by, and empowered by, the Holy Spirit. Again, the New Testament contains little hint that this supernatural Spirit empowerment is limited to an elite group of superchristians or that it bears any kind of expiration date.

**

As a child I was exposed to several teachers who taught that God has constrained himself and does no miracles today. And folks who claimed to do the things Jesus promised – like prophesy, heal, speak in other languages, and exorcise demons – were either crazy or hoaxers. That point of view is called cessationism – the belief that miracles ceased in the early years of the Christian era. But thankfully several events happened throughout my life that prevented me from totally buying into this teaching.

I vividly remember a Bible class I attended when I was a fifth grader. The regular teachers were gone, and instead we were being instructed by a long-time missionary to Brazil. He sat in a metal folding chair, crossed his long thin legs and began describing some of the things he and his fellow missionaries had experienced in South America. One story in particular was set inside an inner city in Brazil. The missionary told of one of his associates who walked into a dimly-lit fortune-teller's shop and noticed a man sitting cross-legged on the floor. The man on the floor started yelling and freaking out. He screamed, his eyes wide and wild, "I know who you are! You have the Spirit of God in you!" Thinking quickly, this missionary, who likely did not believe in demonic possession until that point, rebuked the evil spirit and set about exorcizing the man.

I was captivated by this story. I had always been fascinated by the supernatural, but my Bible teachers had told me the age of devils and angels and miracles was long over. Here was evidence to the contrary.

The missionary moved back to the States and we became good friends. I never forgot his story. And because I believed it I never fully embraced cessationism. Although miracles seemed to have grown rare (at least where I lived), I surmised they still happened somewhere. Perhaps in places where the gospel was new and fresh, and where miraculous signs were most needed to confirm the gospel.

***

The most likely reason why many Christians disbelieve in modern miracles is that they simply haven't seen them. The probable reason they haven't seen miracles is because the spirit of religion has infiltrated the churches and trained God's people to suppress the Holy Spirit. God likes to work through people with great faith in his power. If we lack faith in the miraculous, then the miraculous is unlikely to happen. And even when it does happen, we may fail to see it for what it is.

The New Testament explicitly warns God's people not to narrow their vision of what his Spirit can accomplish. Paul cautioned the Christians in Thessalonica not to "quench the Spirit" or "extinguish the Spirit's fire." (1 Thessalonians 5:19). He told them not to "despise prophecies," but to "test everything" and hold on to what's good. (1 Thessalonians 5:20-21). He instructed the Corinthian Christians, "be eager to prophesy, and do not forbid speaking in tongues." (1 Corinthians 14:28). He warned another church not to "grieve the Holy Spirit of God." (Ephesians 4:30). The writer of Hebrews also says the "Spirit of grace" can be "outraged" or "insulted." (Hebrews 10:29).

The beautiful truth is that God is close to us. He is alive and active. He hears our prayers and acts at the appropriate time. And if we want him to use us in crazy ways and do things that hit people with supernatural power, he is waiting and willing to make it happen. I believe that if we ask for the supernatural, as Jesus says, we shall receive (Matthew 7:7).

But again, even though I always believed miracles were possible, I didn't know what doing them would look like in real life. I had no training in praying in the Spirit, nor in healing people, nor in doing any of the things God does that seem out of this world. Although I believed my private prayers were effective, my engagement with the supernatural did not go much further.

Here, one section of the New Testament becomes especially important.

***

In light of the fact that supernatural gifts were available to all Christians, Paul gave the Christians in Corinth a sort of instruction manual on how to capitalize on those gifts in their assemblies. This is found in First Corinthians chapters 12-14. Spiritual gifts, Paul explains, are heterogeneous:

Now there are different gifts, but the same Spirit. There are different ministries, but the same Lord. And there are different activities, but the same God activates each gift in each person. (HCSB).

Having established that God gives each person different blessings, powers, skills and responsibilities, Paul rattles off a list of spiritual gifts:

to one is given a message of wisdom through the Spirit,

to another, a message of knowledge by the same Spirit,

to another, faith by the same Spirit,

to another, gifts of healing by the one Spirit,

to another, the performing of miracles,

to another, prophecy,

to another, distinguishing between spirits,

to another, different kinds of languages,

to another, interpretation of languages.

But one and the same Spirit is active in all these, distributing to each person as He wills. (HCSB).

So it's all in God's hands. All Christians, Paul says, were "made to drink of one Spirit." But the Lord has downloaded into each believer a unique set of qualities and skills. It's like, as Paul says, a body. Bodies have lots of different parts with different functions, and the parts all work together to actualize the mind's will.

In terms of these functions, Paul says that God has given the church:

first apostles, second prophets,

third teachers, next miracles,

then gifts of healing, helping,

managing, various kinds of languages.

At this point in reading First Corinthians, I might be tempted to whine and say why hasn't God made me one of these people? Paul responds:

Are all apostles? Are all prophets?

Are all teachers? Do all do miracles?

Do all have gifts of healing?

Do all speak in other languages?

Do all interpret? (HCSB).

The implied answer to these rhetorical questions is no. Not everyone has the same gift or gifts. Nevertheless, Paul encourages his readers to "desire the greater gifts." (1 Corinthians 12:31).

That's where I am right now. I can identify gifts that I solidly possess. And I can identify other gifts that I want desperately, but that I am only beginning to experience. As I'll explain later, God has given me the gifts of wisdom, faith, fearlessness, and love. I think I may also have a gift of communication, but you can judge for yourself. People with prophetic gifts have confirmed each of these gifts in me. They've told me that I've been given compassion and supernatural knowledge, and that I'll be given a great gift of gift-giving. I am truly humbled and blessed by these gifts, and I cannot wait to see how God continues to use them to bless people all over the world.

But I also pray almost daily for God to ignite in me the gifts of prophecy and healing. I want to be able to help people even more! Yes, I may possess a spiritual gift of compassion, but that compassionate spirit makes me wish I could free people from their physical and spiritual afflictions with the power of a single prayer and the loving touch of my hand. I want God to tell me things about people that they don't even know about themselves, so this knowledge can set them free from their psychological chains. I've seen brothers and sisters do these things. I want to make the same kind of difference.

But I realize that I have nothing to complain about, because as Paul explains in chapter thirteen of First Corinthians, the greatest spiritual gift is love. The gifts of tongue-speaking, of prophecy, and even of supernatural gift-giving are all worthless if unaccompanied by love. (1 Corinthians 13:1-3). Paul then beautifully details the essential qualities of love and remarks that

Love never fails.

But where there are prophecies, they will cease;

where there are tongues, they will be stilled;

where there is knowledge, it will pass away.

For we know in part and we prophesy in part,

but when completeness comes, what is in part disappears.

When I was a child, I talked like a child, I thought like a child, I reasoned like a child.

When I became a man, I put the ways of childhood behind me.

For now we see only a reflection as in a mirror;

then we shall see face to face.

Now I know in part;

then I shall know fully, even as I am fully known.

And now these three remain: faith, hope and love.

But the greatest of these is love. (1 Corinthians 13:8-13 NIV).

This is a great passage about how love is the greatest gift. But I've got to pause for a moment because some people have misconstrued these words to suggest that God stopped fueling spiritual gifts some time near the end of the first century A.D. Here are the key words again, in a different translation:

Love never ends. But as for prophecies, they will come to an end; as for tongues, they will cease; as for knowledge, it will come to an end. For we know only in part, and we prophesy only in part; but when the complete comes, the partial will come to an end. . . . For now we see in a mirror, dimly, but then we will see face to face. Now I know only in part; then I will know fully, even as I have been fully known.

Paul here says that prophecies, tongues, and supernatural knowledge are "partial." And that's undoubtedly true. No prophet has received a full revelation of everything. People with God-given knowledge don't understand *all* God's mysteries. God only gives people the knowledge and words he knows they need in a given situation. So, the gifts are "partial" or "incomplete." But Paul looks forward to a time when "completion" or "perfection" (or that which is "complete" or "perfect" or "fully mature") arrives. What is he talking about here?

69

I think the "completion" or "perfection" Paul anticipates is the post-resurrection experience he describes two chapters later in First Corinthians. In chapter 15, Paul gives a glimpse of what believers can expect after the return of Christ and the resurrection of the dead. At that time, all God's enemies will be destroyed, even death. (1 Corinthians 15:24-26). Paul focuses on what believers' physical resurrected bodies will be like. He says we will trade a mortal body for an immortal body; a dishonorable body for a glorious body; a weak body for a powerful body. (1 Corinthians 15:42-44, 51-55). In Paul's mind then, "completion" or "perfection" is what arrives when Christ returns and the dead are raised. At that point, all of God's enemies are defeated, the curse is reversed, and God's people live forever with their creator. (See Romans 8:18-23).

I think some of my spiritual predecessors were searching for a biblical passage to justify their belief that God's supernatural gifts had vanished from the church. Because First Corinthians 13:10 talked about gifts "coming to an end," this passage seemed to fit the bill. But they had to interpret "completion" or "perfection" as something that occurred in the past. So, for some interpreters "perfection" became the completion of the New Testament (whether you pinpoint that time as the day Revelation was written in the A.D. 90s or when the 27 books were collected as one authoritative volume around A.D. 367). And for some other interpreters, "completion" arrived at some point in the past when the church itself reached some state of maturity.

But when Paul talks about replacing the partial with the complete in First Corinthians 13, he isn't talking about trading in spiritual gifts for a state of un -giftedness. Paul's looking to trade in partial knowledge for complete knowledge. He wants to swap out partial supernatural language skills for unhindered communication. He wants to upgrade from partial prophecy to a full-frontal experience of the divine. The "ceasing" of the "partial" in First Corinthians 13 isn't a trading-down, but a trading-up! "For now we see only a reflection as in a mirror," he says, but "then we shall see face to face." "Now I know in part," he says, but "then I shall know fully." So, Paul says to his original readers, why get so worked up over your individual supernatural gifts when before long we will all be resurrected and receive knowledge and power beyond what we can imagine?

God's intention, as explained in First Corinthians 13, is that his supernatural gifts will continue to bless the church until his second coming when these limited gifts become obsolete. But the gifts lose their potency without love. God gives the gifts only so that those who carry the gifts can use them to benefit others.

***

Let me make a few other points while we're on the subject of miracles and spiritual gifts. First, Paul does not distinguish in his lists of gifts between what some folks might call "miraculous" or "non-miraculous" gifts. Or between "sign" gifts and non-sign gifts. The ability to give generously and the ability to heal a broken bone with a touch are both extraordinary. The ability to love difficult people and the ability to see their secrets are both beyond normal human experience. When we separate the gifts into classes and say that some continue today, but others do not, then we go beyond the scriptures. When believers do extraordinary things that demonstrate God's love, then the Spirit's gifts are operating, regardless of whether modern people would characterize the result as "against nature." Being selfless is itself, after all, against human nature.

Second, I also don't think Paul's lists of spiritual gifts are intended to be exhaustive, or that there is no overlap between the gifts. You may be gifted in ways that don't fit neatly into one of the categories, and your gifts may evolve over time. All of this is fine once we accept that God's in control.

Third, God, as the gift-giver, often tells his people when it is or is not appropriate to use a gift. Take healing, for example. Some people who disbelieve in contemporary healing say that if the gift of healing really existed, then why don't the healers go into the hospitals and clear them out? What this argument overlooks is that in scripture and throughout the history of God's people, healers generally only heal (and prophets only prophecy) when God tells them to. The people who have these gifts tend to be particularly sensitive to God's leading. Although there are occasions in scripture when Jesus or one of his apostles would heal large groups of people (see Acts 5:12-16), this is not the norm. Typically, the biblical healer singles out a particular person to receive the miracle. In other words, it happens selectively.

For example, Paul's friend Epaphroditus became so sick he nearly died. (Philippians 2:25-28). Another friend, Trophimus, fell ill, and Paul had to leave him behind. (2 Timothy 4:20). Paul was an incredible healer. (See Luke 6:17-19; Acts 19:11-12). Why didn't he heal these friends of his? I suspect it's because God had not told him to. Elijah and Elisha were also great healers, but they also only performed miracles for select individuals. (See Luke 4:24-27). Even with Jesus, there were times when scripture says he was unable to heal. In Matthew 13:58 and Mark 6:5, Jesus's ability to heal people was limited because of the people's lack of trust in him. In Matthew 17:14-20, the disciples' ability to exorcise was limited because the disciples lacked faith. In Mark 9:24-29, the disciples were unable to cast out a demon because they had not been praying.

God knows the best times for healing and prophecy, and he instructs his servants when to act. The person who bears the gift must still agree to act (1 Corinthians 14:32), but unless God instigates the miracle and the servant follows God's lead, then things deviate from God's design.

Fourth, I believe that prophecy and supernatural knowledge exist today. But this does nothing to undermine the authority and centrality of scripture. Scripture is special. The books of the Old and New Testaments were collected and preserved by God's people through the providence of God. As a member of the ancient church, I take it as an article of faith that the scriptures contain everything believers need to know to live a life animated by the indwelling Christ. I strive to honor and obey them, to live in scripture's world and scripture's story.

Although scripture contains prophecies and knowledge from God, new prophecies and knowledge do not supplant scripture. In fact, if they contradict scripture, we must reject them. When I have seen prophecy in use, the message tends to be specific and circumscribed.

Prophetic messages are designed to encourage or convict a particular individual or a particular local church. That's how Paul describes the activity of prophets in Christian gatherings in First Corinthians 14:22-25. Here, Paul paints a picture of how an unbeliever who visits the group will hear the prophets exposing his "secret thoughts." The visitor, confronted with this supernatural knowledge, becomes convicted of his sin and falls to his knees in worship, saying "God is truly here among you."

For other examples of prophetic activity, you might think about how Jesus sometimes knew what his opponents were thinking. (Luke 5:22). Or about how he knew details of the Samaritan woman's personal life although he'd never met her before. (John 4:16 -19). Insights like this are the kinds of signals that prophetically gifted people receive from God. You might also look to the book of Acts and see how prophets told Paul specific details about his future (Acts 21:4, 10-11). As for Paul himself, he experienced comforting visions of Christ (Acts 18:9-10), received directions from God in dreams (Acts 16:9-10) or in trances (Acts 22:17-21), and was given insights into the future (Acts 20:22-23; 27:21-26). So when I talk about prophecy, these are the sorts of messages and insights I'm talking about. They have nothing to do with supplanting scripture.

***

Return with me now to the world of First Corinthians chapters 12-14. When believers get together and activate their spiritual gifts in love, they can accomplish great things. That's why it was so important in the early church that believers in the assembly were allowed to take turns speaking and sharing the things the Spirit had given them. Here is what happened in first-century church meetings, as Paul describes it:

What should be done then, my friends? When you come together, each one has a hymn, a lesson, a revelation, a tongue, or an interpretation. Let all things be done for building up. If anyone speaks in a tongue, let there be only two or at most three, and each in turn; and let one interpret. But if there is no one to interpret, let them be silent in church and speak to themselves and to God. Let two or three prophets speak, and let the others weigh what is said. If a revelation is made to someone else sitting nearby, let the first person be silent. For you can all prophesy one by one, so that all may learn and all be encouraged. And the spirits of prophets are subject to the prophets, for God is a God not of disorder but of peace. (1 Corinthians 14:26-33).

When Christians in the assembly are permitted to prophesy in an orderly manner ("one by one"), the effect is awesome:

[I]f all prophesy, an unbeliever or outsider who enters is reproved by all and called to account by all. After the secrets of the unbeliever's heart are disclosed, that person will bow down before God and worship him, declaring, "God is really among you." (1 Corinthians 14:24-25).

This passage is a vivid portrait of what I've experienced when prophets have spoken to me at Spirit-filled churches. Done correctly in love, personal prophecy can send shockwaves of truth through a person's psyche, making room for the transforming power of the love of Christ to generate wholeness and peace amid a person's inner chaos.

But it takes a bit of courage, founded in love, to invite the Holy Spirit to take the reins of worship.

Let me be clear about one point I'm trying to make from First Corinthians 12-14. There is nothing wrong with asking God to give you spiritual gifts! Do you want to see people healed? Ask for it! Do you want God to tell you things you can't uncover by your own reasoning? Ask him for it! It's what Paul encourages people to do in First Corinthians 14:1. "Pursue love and desire spiritual gifts," Paul says, "and above all that you may prophesy." When I ask God for the gift of prophecy, I am directly heeding the call of this verse.

What I wanted you to see through this whirlwind tour of some New Testament passages is the importance and prominence of the Holy Spirit. He is a key player in the biblical narrative. He empowered Jesus, he empowered the apostles, and he wants to empower you. It's the Spirit who keeps the story of God's people moving from the life of Christ all the way to the end of time. There is no clear indication in the New Testament that the Spirit had plans to leave the earth after a few years or that the Spirit's supernatural gifts carried expiration dates. In fact, the Spirit has a critical role in God's plan to unshackle humanity.

Embracing the contemporary experience of the Holy Spirit makes it harder for the spirit of religion and legalism to take root. Yes, Spirit-filled churches can be hyper-religious and legalistic. Spirit-filled people can get trapped in sin. Even Spirit-filled people (like the recipients of the letters of Paul and John) must remain vigilant against error. They must study the scriptures, and keep their eyes on Jesus.

But what I've found through my journey is that James 4:8 is tangibly true: "Draw near to God, and he will draw near to you." I have chased God all my life, seldom knowing just how close we could actually be. And, perhaps it was my times of darkness (including my atheism and the struggles involving my wife's health that I'll disclose later) that gave me my powerful thirst for the presence of God's Spirit.

Let's move on to awakening.

Three: Awakening

Sometimes we need to be smacked around a little before we can see things as they really are.

I told you at the end of chapter one about how I became an atheist after earning two Bible degrees. My atheism evolved into agnosticism, which basically meant I refused to definitively believe or disbelieve in God. I am convinced that my loss of faith was actually a crucial step in God's plan to draw me back to him. I needed to approach Jesus again with a clean slate – without all the religious baggage I'd accumulated through my early churchgoing days.

How could an egghead like me find his way back to God after he's intellectually rejected the foundational premises of Christianity? Only, I believe, by something supernatural happening.

To explain how I transitioned from agnosticism to faith, I have to tell you part of my other love story – the story of me and my wife.

I abstained from dating in high school because I knew I'd soon be relocating to a college filled with young Christian ladies looking for husbands – a veritable vineyard of inchoate romance. Remaining romantically untethered to my hometown meant I could devote my energies to finding an exemplary college girl to marry me after graduation. My obumbrative dating qualification was that I wanted to find someone more spiritual than myself. I intend no offense, but most church girls appeared to my unseasoned eyes to be shallow and worldly. But I had faith that at a private Christian college I could find a girl who was sincerely and courageously devoted to her Creator. It turns out I met that girl the very first week.

One day the University hauled us freshmen to a local state park and set us free to frolic on our own initiative. I, being an introvert who had grown weary of all the forced social interaction of the first week of school, set off on a solo walk. I followed a trail through the woods that circumnavigated a lake. Halfway around the lake, my beloved and I crossed paths. We became friends.

What attracted me to Lydia was that she wasn't just splashing around in the kiddie pool of spirituality. When it came to serving God, she was determined to jump head-first into the deep end. Lydia aspired to be a missionary to some impoverished third-world hovel where she would live like Mother Theresa, singing while she wiped tears from the horsefly-encrusted eyeballs of starving brown children. Not even I had the guts to make that my career goal. I knew I had found my diamond in the rough, the girl more holy than myself, and I set my face toward wooing her.

But Lydia was reluctant to tether herself to a man who might get in the way of achieving her dream. Although lots of guys had the hots for Lydia, she rebuffed us all. Lydia refused to be anyone's girlfriend. I did my very best. In fact, when I traveled to Israel during my second year of college I placed a written prayer inside a crack in the Wailing Wall that Lydia would be my wife someday. Although she clearly fancied me and I certainly adored her, her refusal to "date" made me so frustrated that to save my sanity I eventually broke off contact with her completely.

Years passed with Lydia and I seeing little of each other. We graduated and went our separate ways.

Three years after I graduated with my master's degree (and then became an agnostic), Lydia and I unexpectedly crossed paths again. A friend of mine who was a missionary to Russia had just returned to Tennessee, and was lodging at another friend's house in

Knoxville. That friend, without telling me, also invited Lydia to visit. I was shocked to see her there. We ended up staying until the next day, and my interest in her was rekindled. After I returned home I wrote her to arrange more time together. She asked what my intentions were. She didn't want to be just friends. I told her I was now "ripe for the plucking" if she wanted me.

Less than six weeks later we were married.

Everything clicked together so beautifully and so rapidly, I could not deny the feeling that providence had guided everything into place. My prayer at the Wailing Wall had been answered. I felt then that God was at work in a personal and existential way. Prayers from years ago were materializing in such a compelling fashion that my agnosticism slid off of me like a snake shedding its skin. I was in love with Lydia. But even more importantly, I was in love with God. Where before I had merely believed, now I loved. Like my transition to atheism, the change was essentially instantaneous.

***

By his grace and through the work of his Spirit, God had rescued me from the spirit of religion and brought me into a more relational kind of faith. I felt loved, and I loved him back. After all, he had given me what I most wanted, my beautiful bride. This was the first part of my new awakening.

And my bibliolatry was gone forever. I am still in love with the Bible, but I now appreciate it for what it is – a tool. God in his triune majesty is the focus of my religion. Not the book, no matter how great it might be. Exalting Christ himself to the throne of my life (in place of the book) has been liberating.

But my reorientation has brought into sharp relief a problem among my evangelical egghead peers. So many arguments among evangelicals revolve around the minutiae of what's written in the book, and in what ways exactly the book is authoritative and what inspiration means. I don't care nearly as much about those arguments anymore. I have faith that when I read scripture prayerfully, God can help me read it correctly. In the process, he can even tell me things I would not find on the printed page. And I have humility that God might be revealing truths to other readers that he might not be showing me.

This is not a low view of scripture. The care I take in handling the Bible – including considering historical context and the subtleties of the original languages – should be apparent in how I've written this book.

But Christ himself is truly my focal point now, and arguments over different interpretations among believers will not again take center stage in the way I experience my faith.

The renewed Bren is no longer terrified of misunderstanding scripture or upset by other people's misunderstandings. I no longer feel like the Bible is something I must master. Instead, it is God's word that must master me. I search its pages to see Jesus, not primarily to formulate doctrine or construct theological arguments. Good theology and good teaching flow from knowing the Lord – both through scripture and through living life in his Spirit.

This is a departure from the training I received at church and in college. Leaders in my church would often describe the Bible as the Constitution of Christianity. As such, the entire New Testament (even the parts that were stories and letters) was supposed to be read as a legal document. This mischaracterization of the New Testament as a legal document is a common lie that's foisted on godly people by the malevolent spirit of religion.

When you begin with the assumption that the New Testament is a legal document, then you interpret the New Testament to bend to that presupposition. What I had to discover through my young adulthood was that this underlying assumption was wrong. The New Testament is not a Constitution. It is not a legal document at all. The problem is essentially a confusion of genres.

In fact the New Testament authors pretty much tell their readers not to interpret their work legalistically. "The letter [of law] kills, but the Spirit gives life," Paul says in Second Corinthians 3:6. Don't submit yourself to regulations, he says again in Colossians 2:20-22. But my people wanted so much for the Bible to be a definitive rule book that we downplayed these passages and manhandled some beautiful Scriptures.

The New Testament itself doesn't read like a legal document. It's a collection of stories and letters. And the biblical writers' instructions sometimes change as circumstances change. For example, in First Corinthians 7, Paul tells the widows in northern Greece they should stay unmarried so they'll have more free time to serve the Lord. But then, over a decade later, in First Timothy 5, Paul tells the widows in Ephesus that they should get married so they won't have so much free time to nose around in other peoples' business. So even the apostles' instructions change as circumstances change. The New Testament defies being read as a constitution, as a once-for-all list of rules.

Yes, the New Testament contains myriad commands – most of them carried over from the Hebrew scriptures. But that's not the gist of the document as a whole. Paul, especially in Romans, is adamant that believers have been freed from the law. When believers focus primarily on following rules and getting everything right, we forget the kind of loving parent God actually is. He's quick to forgive. He's not angry at his children. He wants them to find peace and wholeness, not to be burdened and anxious with the threat of punishment. This is the new understanding to which God has awakened me.

I want to be more awake, more aware of God's closeness, and I hope you do too. I pray for awakening for myself. And I pray for awakening for others who are trapped in emaciated versions of the gospel that dissimulate the imminent power of God and the quickening presence of the Spirit.

Sometimes, when asked to lead prayer, I have prayed the following petition from Paul's letter to the Ephesians. I now pray it for you:

I pray that the God of our Lord Jesus Christ, the Father of glory, may give you a spirit of wisdom and revelation as you come to know him, so that, with the eyes of your heart enlightened, you may know what is the hope to which he has called you, what are the riches of his glorious inheritance among the saints, and what is the immeasurable greatness of his power for us who believe, according to the working of his great power. . . .

I pray that, according to the riches of his glory, he may grant that you may be strengthened in your inner be-ing with power through his Spirit, and that Christ may dwell in your hearts through faith, as you are being rooted and grounded in love. I pray that you may have the power to comprehend, with all the saints, what is the breadth and length and height and depth, and to know the love of Christ that surpasses knowledge, so that you may be filled with all the fullness of God.

Now to him who by the power at work within us is able to accomplish abundantly far more than all we can ask or imagine, to him be glory in the church and in Christ Jesus to all generations, forever and ever. Amen. (Ephesians 1:17-19; 3:16-21).

So, that's one awakening that many of us need – an awakening from legalism, from Pharisee religion – an awakening to the gospel that preaches freedom and love and forgiveness for God's children while it also solicits repentance from the unbeliever.

***

Another aspect of becoming a spiritual muscle, part of receiving the "spirit of wisdom and revelation" is not only knowing about God and his ways, but also knowing your enemy.

So I now transition from an awakening to the power and presence of Christ's Spirit to an awakening to the opposition we muscles must face.

Today I am fully invested in aspects of the biblical worldview that I often hesitated to embrace in the past. Do you believe in the resurrection? Do you believe that Peter's shadow healed the sick (Acts 5:15)? Do you believe that Paul healed people by passing out handkerchiefs (Acts 19:12)? Do you believe a legion of demons bodily possessed a herd of pigs (Mark 5)? Do you believe Peter walked on water and Moses parted the sea (all truly the acts of God, or course)? If so, then why not accept that God can do miraculous things today? And why would you be loath to believe that demonic spirits are manipulating people today? Because the concrete effects of malevolent spiritual activity is a well-attested aspect of the biblical world.

The world of the Bible is haunted by waspish incorporeal beings that delight in screwing up people's lives. Many of our human afflictions, from physical ailments to depression to fear to self-criticism, may actually be symptoms of demonic activity.

As a professional and a scholar, I admit I feel uncomfortable typing the preceding sentence. Nevertheless, I have decided to go all-in. If I accept Christ's salvation, I think I also need to accept Christ's own story, and that's a story about God's Son defeating the demonic powers of the Devil. I also accept this supernatural view of the world because I've seen it work.

Let's look now at "possession," and some of the other ways in which the powers of hate afflict God's creation.

The "Legion" narrative is perhaps the most interesting and best-known demonic possession story from the Gospels. It's in Matthew, Mark, and Luke. Notice what the evil spirits say, where the spirits like to live, and how their presence affects the man they chose to inhabit. Here is the story, as told in Luke 8. As Jesus stepped out of a boat onto the shore of the Sea of Galilee,

A man of the city who had demons met him. For a long time he had worn no clothes, and he did not live in a house but in the tombs. When he saw Jesus, he fell down before him and shouted at the top of his voice, "What have you to do with me, Jesus, Son of the Most High God? I beg you, do not torment me" – for Jesus had commanded the unclean spirit to come out of the man. (For many times it had seized him; he was kept under guard and bound with chains and shackles, but he would break the bonds and be driven by the demon into the wilds.) Jesus then asked him, "What is your name?" He said, "Legion"; for many demons had entered him. They begged him not to order them to go back into the abyss.

Now there on the hillside a large herd of swine was feeding; and the demons begged Jesus to let them enter these. So he gave them permission. Then the demons came out of the man and entered the swine, and the herd rushed down the steep bank into the lake and was drowned.

So here we see a full-blown possession. Notice that the demons drove the man to homelessness. They made him antisocial and dangerous. They gave him powers, but he was not able to put those talents (in this case, unusual strength) to good use. The demons were attracted to death. Despite their ferocity and their sheer numbers, all Jesus had to do to drive away the evil spirits was to command them, and they obeyed. I imagine he issued a similar command with Mary Magdalene, who was also oppressed by multiple demons. (Luke 8:2).

There are many manifestations of demonic activity that fall short of full-blown possession like the story of the Legion. The Bible talks about spirits that lie to people, that physically and emotionally torment people, that cause people to lose their love for God, or that make people confused and disoriented.

We're about to survey a bunch of passages from the Bible that depict spirits influencing people. I acknowledge that in some of these passages, the "spirit" could be legitimately interpreted as the person's own spirit, perhaps meaning the person's psyche or mental state or disposition. But other passages are clear references to independent personal beings.

At the outset, please remember that the Bible makes a distinction between illness and demonic afflictions. And the New Testament shows that Jesus and his disciples could heal both kinds of problems. For example, in Matthew 8:16, people bring to Jesus "many who were possessed with demons; and he cast out the spirits with a word, *and* cured all who were sick." Similarly, in Acts 5:16, just as had happened with Jesus, crowds of people gathered around the apostles, "bringing the sick *and* those tormented by unclean spirits, and they were all cured." The disciples' ability to recapitulate Jesus's healings is unsurprising because as early as Matthew 10:1, Jesus granted his disciples "authority over unclean spirits, to cast them out, *and* to cure every disease and every sickness." In each of these passages, demonic affliction and physical ailment are listed separately. Not all afflictions, sicknesses, or neuroses are spiritual in origin. But some of them are.

***

In the Hebrew Bible (Old Testament), vexatious spirits are typically described as coming from the Lord. This initially struck me as quite odd. But to the earliest Hebrew writers, everything was ultimately attributable to God. So these writers did not hesitate to ascribe the origin of evil spirits to the Maker. They weren't as squeamish about that as a modern person might be.

First, the Bible mentions spirits that attack people's minds and emotions. Isaiah prophesies against Israel's enemies that the Lord has poured into them "a *spirit of confusion*" that makes them "stagger [like] a drunkard staggers around in vomit." (Isaiah 19:14). In the American Standard Version, this is a "spirit of perverseness." In another passage, the Lord is said to have poured out "a *spirit of deep sleep*" on Israel's enemies that saps their energy. (Isaiah 28:10). The book of Judges references an "evil spirit" that interfered with the relationship between Israel's king and the men of Shechem, causing the Shechemites to betray the king's trust. (Judges 9:22-24). Numbers chapter five talks about a "*spirit of jealousy*" that "comes upon" a man who believes his wife has committed adultery. The prophet Hosea also speaks twice of a "*spirit of whoredom*" that has led people astray, such that they no longer know their Lord. (Hosea 4:12; 5:4).

One of the most remarkable passages about emotion -attacking spirits concerns Saul, the first king of Israel. David, Saul's future successor to the throne, is a skilled musician whom Saul hires to soothe him with music whenever he's troubled by a vexatious spirit that God sent to punish him. First Samuel 16:14-16 says:

Now the spirit of the Lord departed from Saul, and an evil spirit from the Lord tormented him. And Saul's servants said to him, "See now, an evil spirit from God is tormenting you. Let our lord now command the servants who attend you to look for someone who is skillful in playing the lyre; and when the evil spirit from God is upon you, he will play it, and you will feel better."

So Saul hires David for the job. The text says that "whenever the evil spirit from God came upon Saul, David took the lyre and played it with his hand, and Saul would be relieved and feel better, and the evil spirit would depart from him." (1 Samuel 16:23).

One thing to notice in this story (aside from the ability of good music to ward off evil) is the fact that after a tormenting spirit is driven away, it can return later and resume its mischief. It is like the lesson Jesus told in Matthew 12:43-45:

When the unclean spirit has gone out of a person, it wanders through waterless regions looking for a resting place, but it finds none. Then it says, 'I will return to my house from which I came.' When it comes, it finds it empty, swept, and put in order. Then it goes and brings along seven other spirits more evil than itself, and they enter and live there; and the last state of that person is worse than the first. So will it be also with this evil generation.

This passage is a reminder that freeing a person from the influence of bad spirits (just like recovering from many mental and physical illnesses) can take time. And relapses are possible. If you're helping somebody who's tormented, don't abandon them after they seem healed. Lasting deliverance can require follow-up.

The Bible also talks about spirits that spread false ideas. One interesting story is found in both First Kings 22 and Second Chronicles 18. Here, Micaiah, a good prophet, is speaking to the wicked King Ahab of Israel in the presence of other so-called prophets who habitually tell the king whatever he wants to hear. Micaiah says,

I saw the Lord sitting on his throne, with all the host of heaven standing beside him to the right and to the left of him. And the Lord said, 'Who will entice Ahab, so that he may go up and fall at Ramoth-gilead?' Then one said one thing, and another said another, until a spirit came forward and stood before the Lord, saying, 'I will entice him.' 'How?' the Lord asked him. He replied, 'I will go out and be a lying spirit in the mouth of all his prophets.'

Then the Lord said, 'You are to entice him, and you shall succeed; go out and do it.' So you see, the Lord has put a lying spirit in the mouth of all these your prophets; the Lord has decreed disaster for you.

Micah 2:11 also describes a man with "the *spirit of falsehood*" who pretends to prophesy, but lies.

These lying spirits are not just in the Old Testament, either. In First John 4:6, John says he and the other apostles "know the spirit of truth and *the spirit of error.*" First Timothy 4:1 is also an important passage. Here, Paul tells his apprentice:

Now the Holy Spirit tells us clearly that in the last times some will turn away from the true faith; they will follow deceptive spirits and teachings that come from demons.

The American Standard Version called these spirits "seducing spirits." What specifically do these deceptive spirits teach? "They forbid marriage and demand abstinence from foods, which God created to be received with thanksgiving by those who believe and know the truth." (1 Timothy 4:3). In other words, they teach legalism. Phariseeism. This is what I'm getting at when I talk about the spirit of religion corrupting believers and even whole churches. The urge to flatten scripture into a mere rulebook is not from God, but from the evil powers of the air.

But the effects of evil spirits can go beyond the invisible, doctrinal, and psychological. In the biblical world, spirits can cause physical illness. In Luke 13:11, Jesus meets a woman "with a spirit that had crippled her for eighteen years." The King James Version called this a "*spirit of infirmity*." The English Standard Version calls it a "disabling spirit."

In another New Testament story, a spirit caused a person to suffer deafness, muteness, and convulsions:

"What is all this arguing about?" Jesus asked. One of the men in the crowd spoke up and said, "Teacher, I brought my son so you could heal him. He is possessed by an evil spirit that won't let him talk. And whenever this spirit seizes him, it throws him violently to the ground. Then he foams at the mouth and grinds his teeth and becomes rigid. So I asked your disciples to cast out the evil spirit, but they couldn't do it."

Jesus said to them, "You faithless people! How long must I be with you? How long must I put up with you? Bring the boy to me." So they brought the boy. But when the evil spirit saw Jesus, it threw the child into a violent convulsion, and he fell to the ground, writhing and foaming at the mouth. "How long has this been happening?" Jesus asked the boy's father. He replied, "Since he was a little boy. The spirit often throws him into the fire or into water, trying to kill him. Have mercy on us and help us,

*if you can." "What do you mean, 'If I can'?" Jesus asked.
"Anything is possible if a person believes." The father in-
stantly cried out, "I do believe, but help me overcome my
unbelief!"*

*When Jesus saw that the crowd of onlookers was growing,
he rebuked the evil spirit. "Listen, you spirit that makes
this boy unable to hear and speak," he said. "I command
you to come out of this child and never enter him again!"
Then the spirit screamed and threw the boy into another
violent convulsion and left him. The boy appeared to be
dead. A murmur ran through the crowd as people said,
"He's dead." But Jesus took him by the hand and helped
him to his feet, and he stood up.*

*Afterward, when Jesus was alone in the house with his
disciples, they asked him, "Why couldn't we cast out that
evil spirit?" Jesus replied, "This kind can be cast out only
by prayer."* (Mark 9:16-29) (NLT).

In many manuscripts, Jesus says it's "prayer and fasting" that are required to exorcise a spirit this powerful. This is a reminder that being a powerful muscle
to do God's work requires a strong relationship with
God – the kind we can develop through spiritual dis-
cipline.

The Bible also has references to *"familiar spirits,"*
which ungodly people consult in order to obtain
supernatural knowledge. (Leviticus 20:6; 1 Samuel

28:3; 2 Kings 21:6; 23:4; Isaiah 8:19, etc.). They're in the New Testament, too. In Acts 16:16, the missionaries Paul and Silas are in Philippi in northern Greece when they encounter "a slave-girl who had a *spirit of divination* and brought her owners a great deal of money by fortune-telling."

One component of the worldview of the biblical authors is that there exist two parallel realms that interact with each other – the earthly realm and the heavenly realm. To get a clear picture of this interaction, read through the book of Revelation and notice how events on earth affect events in heaven, and vice -versa. Demonic possession and affliction are manifestations of these two levels of reality colliding.

I understand that this dualistic cosmology is not part of the contemporary western worldview. And the existence of the spirit realm is not subject to empirical verification or testing by the scientific method. But I have chosen not to limit my worldview to things that can only be verified by the conventional sense organs. When it comes to the physical world, I trust science to provide the best answers. But the spirit world is a world grasped only through intuitions, dreams, visions, impressions, and through the rich heritage of spiritual and mystical literature that humankind has cobbled together in awe and fear – most importantly the inspired Bible.

***

What I've found is that by choosing to engage evil and suffering on both fronts – physical and spiritual – I am more effective in fostering healing and reconciliation. After all, choosing to engage people, systems, and events both physically and spiritually is precisely what Christ, the apostles, and the prophets did.

For example, a physician may engage both realms by praying for his patients as he treats them with conventional medicine. A person caring for a sick relative may also ask God to protect the person with his angels and banish any harmful spirits from the house. An activist may work for social change in the political sphere, but also petition God to open the eyes of people in power, and to crush the armies of invisible evil that want to hijack human institutions to breed suffering and hatred. Conversely, a person who typically prays alone for his friends may additionally start sending emails of encouragement to those friends. It's even better to pray for people in person or over the phone. A two-pronged attack can make ministering exponentially more effective because you become invested in the fight in both the visible and invisible realms.

I am not saying that Christians should never seek help from medical doctors, counselors, or psychologists when they suffer physical or mental diseases.

Physical illnesses are real, and can often be treated by altering habits, changing diet, and when absolutely necessary through drugs and other medical treatments. But I now wield an additional treatment method. When it comes to myself and others, I will pray positively for healing and divine assistance, and pray negatively for banishment of evil spiritual influences. I have also found, as James 5:13-18 suggests, that my prayers are more effective when I really put my heart in them and absolutely groan to the Lord.

So, I choose to live in the world of the Bible – the world where Christ has given his children authority over evil spirits. And, although it's off my topic, I might mention that embracing a more supernaturalistic worldview opens you up to a more immediate experience of God in worship. If you go to church expecting God to show up, then you might hear his voice during congregational singing and prayer. As my friend John Mark Hicks likes to write about, you might find yourself transported to the heavenly throne room during worship or suddenly sense the presence of Christ as you celebrate him through the Lord's Supper.

As an example of an intellectual who embraced the spirit-world, consider William Stringfellow, an attorney and theologian who fought for social justice

in the mid-twentieth century. Stringfellow once fa-
mously attempted a long-distance exorcism of Pres-
ident Richard Nixon. The idea struck me as odd at
first, but it's grown on me. The Enemy is certainly interested in corrupting powerful institutions and powerful people, and we should pray for God's angels to
shield our leaders and institutions from corruption.
(1 Timothy 2:1-3). And we should do what we can
to drive out the manifestations of evil – racism, sex-
ism, inequality, callousness, cronyism, and all other
Satanic schemes – from our human institutions. I'm
talking about coupling activism with prayer.

Remember, if you want to be the most powerful muscle for the Lord that you can be, you'd better live in
the reality Paul paints in Ephesians 6:10-18 (NLT):

*A final word: Be strong in the Lord and in his mighty
power. Put on all of God's armor so that you will be able
to stand firm against all strategies of the devil. For we are
not fighting against flesh-and-blood enemies, but against
evil rulers and authorities of the unseen world, against
mighty powers in this dark world, and against evil spirits in the heavenly places.*

*Therefore, put on every piece of God's armor so you will be
able to resist the enemy in the time of evil. Then after the
battle you will still be standing firm. Stand your ground,
putting on the belt of truth and the body armor of God's*

righteousness. For shoes, put on the peace that comes from the Good News so that you will be fully prepared. In addition to all of these, hold up the shield of faith to stop the fiery arrows of the devil. Put on salvation as your helmet, and take the sword of the Spirit, which is the word of God.

Pray in the Spirit at all times and on every occasion. Stay alert and be persistent in your prayers for all believers everywhere.

As this passage says, our struggle is not against "flesh and blood," meaning fellow-humans. People are not your enemies. People are for you to love. Your enemies are spirits and structures of suffering and corruption. So don't aim your arrows at the wrong target. Direct your frustration at the systems and authorities and human social structures that have been corrupted by the Devil, with his seductions and false promises and jealousies and lies.

But don't write off all human structures and systems, either. Even corrupted institutions and social structures, be they government bodies, political parties, churches, or schools, can be redeemed and made healthy once evil has been driven out.

***

My bottom line is that if you believe in the story of Christ as told in the gospels, then you believe in demonic activity. Satan's minions lie to us and torment us and try to undo the work of God wherever it's flourishing. Perhaps it's happening to your right now.

Are there lies you believe about yourself, about your family, about your abilities, your church, your God? You might want to pray for the Lord to reveal any lies you might have internalized. God doesn't tell you things that discourage you or make you afraid or make you feel weak. God doesn't put you down. If you believe things that discourage you or make you feel alone or helpless or afraid, these are lies from the dark side and not the truth. When you perceive one of these lies forming in your mind, I suggest that you call it what it is and banish it with prayer. If you feel a thought coming on that makes you think less of yourself or less of God, label it as a lie and rebuke it. Order it to evacuate your skull in the name of Jesus.

The Devil wants to make people hate themselves, hate their spouses, hate the parents, their children, their leaders. He loves to destroy marriages and spiritual friendships, and he often does it by getting people to believe lies about themselves or about others. In contrast, God is light and truth. He helps us see the value in ourselves and the beauty in people around us. We would all do well to become more adept in distinguishing thoughts that are true and pure from those that cause fear, self-loathing, jealousy, unforgiveness, and the like. As Paul counsels in Second Corinthians 10:3-5:

Indeed, we live as human beings, but we do not wage war according to human standards; for the weapons of our warfare are not merely human, but they have divine power to destroy strongholds. We destroy arguments and every proud obstacle raised up against the knowledge of God, and we take every thought captive to obey Christ.

So, I've talked at length here about demonic forces, but I don't want to dwell on them. Soon, my focus will shift back to the other side of spiritual awareness – awareness of the Spirit and God's angels.

But first I want to talk briefly about being called.

Four: The Call

So, in 2002 I married my dear bride. And the serendipitous way everything fell into place reignited my faith in God. I had run from the Lord, but his Spirit yearned for me so greatly he drew me back to himself. My early intellectual faith had collapsed into faithlessness, and this spiritual vacuum created a space in which a new, existential faith could flourish. I now felt that I knew Christ – not only through the precious biblical texts, but through my inner assurance that his compassionate providence was directing my life. I understood now how close God was, and how patient he is with people. It was as though he communicated these insights directly into my heart through sensations rather than words. I also was becoming a contemplative person. I learned to meditate. I taught myself to be still and just think about Jesus for long periods of time. Being alone with God or with an idea from him is what made me feel like I lived in his presence.

I eventually decided to resume my theological education and earn a master of divinity degree. I figured I was headed toward becoming a theology professor because I loved studying scripture, philosophy, and the writings of the early church fathers.

By the time I graduated from my M.Div. program in 2006, my wife was pregnant with our first of three sons. I had applied to seven different Ph.D. programs, but none of them accepted me. I found out later that there was a problem with the transcripts my school had sent. It was a silly, useless mistake, but I told myself that it must have been providential for a strange random screw-up to prevent me from going into academia at that point. Instead, I obtained a job as a campus minister in Florida.

I was on staff with the campus ministry for three exciting years. I loved working with college students, and I still do. I felt that God has equipped me to teach young adults because I'm comfortable with the spiritual struggles and identity issues that emerging adults invariably face. I enjoy being a safe person who can engage with college students' existential questions without judging them or pressuring them. Because I had the gift of faith, I was confident my students would not lose their connection to Christ in the long run.

Aside from relocating to Florida and acclimating to a new job, our lives changed in another profound way. In April 2008, our twins were born. Fortunately, they were healthy. But they were not easy. One twin had a penchant for near-constant screaming. That's not pleasant. Also, a month after they were born, the other twin got a fever that wouldn't go away. Lydia took the little guy to the hospital, and the doctors ran a lot of invasive tests on him. It was traumatic for Lydia to watch our son suffer, and he ended up spending three days in the hospital.

On the little dude's second night of recovery, I was keeping him company in his hospital room. I sat in a vinyl chair beside the clear plastic box in which he slept. The night grew late, and I was unable to sleep.

Suddenly, around 2 a.m., I heard an audible male voice. The voice enunciated a single sentence. It said, "You should go to law school."

I could tell the sound didn't come from the hospital intercom. Also, it wasn't just that I heard it with my ears, but I could feel the voice in my brain. My right temporal lobe, to be exact. But wherever it came from, the voice had my attention.

I had never heard a disembodied voice like that before. And I had never thought about going to law school before. I happened to have a laptop computer with me, so I removed it from its bag and immediately started researching law schools and legal careers over the hospital wi-fi. The more I read about the law, the more I felt it suited me.

I had been given a calling. I had heard the voice of the Lord, and I knew I had to obey.

I applied to two schools, but I knew Vanderbilt was where I wanted to go. It was a great school, and it was near my family, and my father had told me that he'd help me if I ever wanted to get a doctorate, which in this case meant they'd let me live in their old house. Thanks, mom and dad!

My biggest hurdle to getting into Vanderbilt was the Law School Admissions Test, or LSAT. Vanderbilt's an elite school, and I knew I needed a near-perfect score to compete with those applicants who, unlike me, had attended top-ranked undergraduate schools. The verbal portions of the LSAT were easy, but the test also has a section of so-called logic "games" that gave me all sorts of problems. To compensate for my dullness in the logic-games category, I bought several books of questions and practiced every day for weeks prior to the LSAT.

Then there was a glitch. As the test approached, I felt my body giving out on me. I was sore and spacy and lethargic. And an enormous boil appeared on my

upper back and grew very red and sore and uncomfortable. I had developed both mononucleosis and
an infected sebaceous cyst. But I was able to make it
through the LSAT. And I even got the killer score I
needed to break into Vanderbilt. A month later I got
my acceptance packet in the mail.

God had called me, and I had answered, and he'd
helped me answer the call even when physical road-
blocks stood in my way. He came through for me,
and I haven't looked back.

***

God offers general calls to everybody, and also sometimes specific calls. Many of these general calls are
found in scripture. We know God's will or desire for
all people is that we live lives of integrity, outstand-
ing ethics, and service to others. (See 1 Thessalonians
4:3, 5:18; 1 Peter 2:15). God wants everyone's heart to
reflect the power of his love, to embrace life and the
endless possibilities he offers. He wants everyone's
mind to be freed from lies and from shackles that
inhibit growth and joy. He wants to see us frolic toward him in spontaneous worship and to one day live
forever with him as his friends in paradise.

Does every person have a specific calling from God?
I don't have enough information yet to know if that's

the case. God called Abraham to uproot himself and move to a new country. God called Gideon to lead an idiosyncratic army. God called Samuel to change the trajectory of Israel in a single generation. God called Mary to be the mother of his child. Christ called the twelve to be his personal disciples, to follow his lead as teachers and exorcists. God called Paul to take Christ's message to the pagans and philosophers he previously considered unclean. He has called me to be a lawyer and a writer.

But I also know that, even without a specific calling like the voice I heard in the hospital in 2008, I would still have a smorgasbord of clear ministries in front of me. I have the ministry of being a father and husband, which I ignore at my own peril. I am a minister to my friends, each of whom has his or her own unique struggle. There is no dearth of opportunities for service at my church. I'm sure I could please my Lord by choosing any of these ministries.

I've often prayed since law school for God to show me what specific type of lawyer I should become, or what specific job to seek out. But more than one prophetically-gifted brother has told me that God has prepared several paths for me, and I can choose whichever one I wish. The choice, God's said, is mine. It's not the case that you only have one thing you're designed to do, and you fail if you choose something else.

Maybe you feel that God has called you to do something specific. If you have answered the call, and the calling suits your talents and disposition, then good for you. Or, perhaps you feel called to do something specific, but you have some hesitation. There is no harm in seeking wise advice. Solicit the prayers of the wisest and holiest people you know so they can either confirm your calling or perhaps set you on a better path.

But maybe you don't feel called to anything in particular. Some people feel this way and get frustrated about it. If that's you, it's okay. Just be who you are. Do whatever God sets in front of you. You don't have to impress God. He already knows everything about you. He already likes you and loves you. No doubt he's pleased you're even thinking about the subject. Just tell the Lord that if he wants to call you into a particular mission, you are ready and willing to answer his call.

When God does give you an assignment, be sure to do it. Refusing the call can have harsh consequences. Consider Jonah. Jonah rejected the mission God gave him, and it led to a very harrowing and traumatic experience at sea. Also, do you remember the story of my friend Jon and his three companions from Chapter One? Their visit to the wreckage of the World Trade Center the day after the 9/11 attacks is a stirring testimony to how God works in the world. Jon is now an associate minister and school teacher who touches lives for Jesus every day. It's not unusual at all see him give prophetic encouragement to someone or to place his hands on a suffering stranger and pray for healing.

But Jon's three friends no longer believe the Spirit miraculously works and speaks and heals. They've returned to the cessationist thinking of their religious roots. When they talk about their 9/11 experience, they chalk it up to luck and random chance. I won't get into the details of their personal struggles, but their lives lack the joy and spiritual health that radiates from Jon and his family. Jon has remained close to God and has spiritually prospered. His friends lost their belief in the supernatural and their power has withered. Our awareness of the indwelling life of Christ can fade away if we do not nurture it.

***

After being called to law school, I also strayed from my path. After our son left the hospital, life went back to normal. My focus returned to growing the campus ministry and to the lives of the students. Applying to law school shifted to the back burner of the stovetop of my mind. One day, spiritually exhausted from both ministry and raising three tiny striplings, I went for a walk at a wildlife refuge. I was following a trail that was built on a levee, with alligator-infested waters to my right and to my left. But after walking a few minutes, I noticed that far ahead of me that the path was blocked. A group of wild boars was eating a dead deer! Right in the middle of the levee trail. There was no way I could get around them, and I was certainly not eager to interact with probably the meanest species of wild animals in the American southeast. I had no choice but to turn around.

Kind of spooked by the experience, I returned to my car and drove to a Walmart store in a nearby town. I have no idea why I felt I needed to go to Walmart. I wanted to spend time outdoors with God, with nothing but the sky and the sea and the grasses and the gators to keep us company. Walmart was kind of the opposite of that. But as I walked toward the entrance of the store, one of the college students in my campus ministry sauntered out. We ended up going to a pizza shop together. He asked me how my law school plans were going, and I admitted that they'd fizzled out.

This student had heard my story of being called to law school, and that day he set me straight. He gave me the most effective pep-talk of my life. It was only after that experience that I started filling out law school applications. I had wandered toward the precipice of denying the call, but God didn't let me off the hook it. And to nudge me back on path, he recruited some wild animals and used a student to teach his teacher.

I also believe that if you've wandered from your calling, God is willing to give you another chance. Maybe that's even why I'm writing this book for you now. What great thing are you poised to do, but you just haven't had the courage to pull the trigger?

The idea of calling is important because God himself is on a mission. And he loves to delegate specific tasks to his people and then to equip them to obliterate those goals with extreme prejudice. Please allow me now to ruminate on this idea of God's mission.

***

The God I worship is a God who wants something.

Even before the universe was born, God was love. Because God is triune, there is eternal love among the community of the Father, Son, and Spirit. But this Godhead is so overflowing with love, God wanted to enlarge the family. That's why the world was made. God wasn't lonely, but he did, like most parents, want to experience the joy of having children. There's no other good biblical explanation for why he would sculpt this world and season it with human beings. We are what he wants.

But what love wants in return is more love. And love must be voluntary. For God to enjoy genuine love from humans, this required that humans have a legitimate opportunity to choose. That's why it was necessary for man to obtain the knowledge of good and evil. Without the knowledge of the alternatives to walking with God, there is no choice. Without choice, there is no love. And what God wants is to bask in love – to give and receive love, with joy, for all eternity.

God therefore designed a world in which the beings he designed to love him could choose God – choose love and choose life – or they could choose death and separation. The story of the Bible is the story of God's own mission to woo each of us into a love affair with him.

God chose to heal the distance between him and ourselves by calling a family – a nation – to experience him personally and then tell the world who the Creator was and what the Creator liked. That is the story of Israel, God's "kingdom of priests," which

God called to educate and heal the heathen nations around them. By preserving the crucial truths about God through their scripture and worship, the nation of the Hebrews prepared the way for God to demonstrate his love in the most radical way possible through Jesus Christ.

The death and resurrection of Christ accomplished several things. Christ was an atoning sacrifice, a scapegoat who absorbed the collective sins of humanity, thus revealing the will to forgive that lies at the tender heart of God. Christ's act of love opened the door to reuniting God and people with the same freedom and intimacy they experienced in the Garden of Eden. Christ also conquered the powers of evil through his death, and exposed the political and religious structures of human existence as the frauds that they so often are. The State and the Church are not our savior, and we know it because the State and the church worked together to kill the Messiah. But in addition to bringing atonement for sin, defeating the devil, and exposing the worldly powers in his death, Christ also demonstrated the unfathomable depths of God's love for lowly human beings. God loved us so much he was willing to empty himself in the incarnation, to live a life of lowly service, and then to die a dolorous death. Surely the only appropriate response to a gesture of such painful beauty is to fall in love with the Being who did it.

When we become one with Christ, we join his mission and his movement. We share his objectives. It becomes our life's goal to heal broken relationships. The end game of all ministries and callings is to help people fall in love with their Lord.

Oh, God, if only you would give me syllables to paint a word picture that captures your achingly beautiful love! If only I could be your match-maker and that my humble writings could cause lonely hearts to gravitate to your heart! Give me Spirit, give me words. Light my keystrokes on fire so the flame can spread to the readers!

There is more. In addition to being called to love, all humans are also called to rule. Part of your calling is to understand and seize your identity in Christ. Let's return to the before-and-after picture of redeemed human beings from Ephesians chapter two:

You were dead through the trespasses and sins in which you once lived, following the course of this world, following the ruler of the power of the air, the spirit that is now at work among those who are disobedient. All of us once lived among them in the passions of our flesh, following the desires of flesh and senses, and we were by nature children of wrath, like everyone else.

But God, who is rich in mercy, out of the great love with which he loved us even when we were dead through our trespasses, made us alive together with Christ – by grace you have been saved – and raised us up with him and seated us with him in the heavenly places in Christ Jesus, so that in the ages to come he might show the immeasurable riches of his grace in kindness toward us in Christ Jesus. For by grace you have been saved through faith, and this is not your own doing; it is the gift of God – not the result of works, so that no one may boast. For we are what he has made us, created in Christ Jesus for good works, which God prepared beforehand to be our way of life.

This passage gives me strength when life gets hard, especially when I let myself down. I must remember that I'm a resurrected being. I can endure anything if I can just remember my identity in Christ. I am no longer a walking dead man, slogging through a meaningless life of doing whatever my body and my feelings tell me to do.

No! God has raised me from that existential tomb! Not only that, God has exalted me to heaven. I reign with Christ right now. You too, believer, are a king or queen of the universe, enthroned with Christ in God. You have been saved. And in this context, the one who saved us is God in Christ, and what we've been saved from is the old dead life – the life of loneliness and meaninglessness and disappointment. He's saved us from the worst part of ourselves so we could become our highest, greatest selves in him.

And what is our lifestyle once we've embraced our true identity as spiritual royalty? We live a life of good works, just as Jesus did. Just as we were created to do. We become part of God's body, his muscles working on earth. And it feels good.

The person who walks in this identity walks in a spirit of freedom and gratitude because that new identity is like being rescued from drowning. The salvation Paul speaks of – being saved from an animalistic lifestyle – is the result of grace (God's generosity) and faithfulness. I believe the "faith" Paul mentions here is Christ's faithfulness. The word "faith" (*pistis* in Greek) doesn't typically mean belief in the intellectual sense. The word refers to trust and dependability. We have this great gift – salvation – because God was generous and Christ was faithful and dependable. Jesus was faithful and dependable even to the point of becoming human and dying in pain and injustice. He performed the heart-breaking story of God's love on the theater stage of human history.

When I awaken to who I am and to what my calling is, the thing that remains is empowerment. A muscle must be made strong. If you know about muscles, you know that what makes them grow harder and stronger is strain and tissue damage. God empowers us, but we often have to suffer before we can fully accept that gift. It is to this process that we now turn.

Five: Empowerment

Our first five years of parenthood almost killed us. We love our boys, but they were not the quiet, easy type. It was like a destructive force of nature had moved into our home. But what made this period feel like our valley of the shadow of death was Lydia's depression.

There's nothing you can really say or do to make a depressed person happy. When the clouds of despair roll in, you just have to ride out the ensuing storm. And depression's wingman is insomnia. For Lydia, sleep became as elusive as the Yeti. The insomnia left her mind brittle and vulnerable. Droves of dark, angry, accusatory thoughts would invade her consciousness and fasten themselves like ticks. Although Lydia knew intellectually she was blessed in many ways, to her despondent heart everything around her bore the stench of death and betrayal. And she was angry about it. Angry at me, at the kids, at our relatives, at the people at church. She felt wretched and weak, and she imagined that people were judging her a failure. She lost friendships. We became reclusive and withdrawn. Sometimes I'd be at law school and I'd get a call from Lydia, and she'd be sobbing and kids would be screaming in the background, and she'd say I don't know what to do, I just can't take this anymore.

And I prayed. I'd put my hand on her and pray for healing, but healing never seemed to come.

But then a splinter of light began breaking through the clouds of despair. Lydia suddenly began writing songs. Songs of faith and hope and triumph in Christ. Previously, I was the musician and songwriter in the family, and she was the one who drew and sculpted. But without warning, Lydia started writing multiple songs a day. She'd be awake in the night, and to ward off the hateful voices, songs started flowing out of her. They came effortlessly. They were catchy. They communicated hope. And each one was different. It was like God was beginning to work in her.

But new, brighter phase in our life would not be fully birthed until the end of 2013.

***

Our best friends from college had started attending a new weird church south of Nashville. Week after week, our friends told us amazing stories about the people there. They told us about the astonishingly insightful prayers people had prayed for them. And they'd seen healings, too. One night I decided I *had* to visit that church, even if it meant leaving Lydia alone at home.

On the first week of December 2013, I attended one of this church's three-hour services. I sat by myself in the middle of the auditorium – a silent observer surrounded by mostly artsy-looking young people. College students, hipsters, musicians, and graphic designers seemed to flock to this group.

First, the worship band played for an hour. I knew none of the songs. The music was slow and kind of repetitive. People swayed and raised their hands. I found out later that this was "soaking" music – designed to help people slip into a relaxed and contemplative state of mind.

I'd heard from my friends that this church practiced prophetic prayer. The church has multiple prayer teams. The teams at this church were groups of two people, usually a man and a woman, who stood at the front of the meeting room to pray specific personal private prayers for the people who came forward and asked for them. I was eager to get this kind of prayer. What would the Lord tell me? Would it be for real? I decided I wasn't going to go forward unless I felt the Lord compelled me.

After a guest speaker preached for almost an hour, the pastor made an invitation for people to approach the prayer teams. The time felt right; I practically raced to the front of the auditorium.

I was prayed over by a skinny young white man with dreadlocks, glasses, and a plaid flannel shirt. His partner was a female nursing student. Neither one had ever met me or heard anything about me. They asked my name and what I wanted prayers for. I told them I had no special request: just tell me whatever God wants me to hear. What happened next changed my family's future.

The young man laid one hand on my shoulder and placed the fingers of his other hand gently against my sternum. For a moment he was quiet. The church band played softly in the background. But then he spoke, and what he said revealed things about me. I'll tell you some of it.

He told me he knew my heart was full of love and compassion. He remarked that I had known since childhood that God had loved me, and that I'd always felt secure in God's love. This was true, and would not have been true of everybody there. Then he told me my gift was sharing that divine love with others. He said that God was going to give me more boldness to do so. The young man said I had family members who he described as "conservative or liturgical." Again, the "conservative" part was true for me, but would not have been true of most people at that church. He said God would soon enable me to share God's love story with these conservative relatives.

Then the young lady addressed me. She said God gave her an image. The image she saw was a heart, my heart. She saw it by itself – hovering, I imagine. My heart was pumping and pumping and blood was shooting out of it. She interpreted the vision. She said that all the blood coming out of my heart meant that I was capable of giving and giving and I would never run out. Just as my heart never runs out of blood, I'd never run out of gifts to give. She said I might not be able to give so liberally yet. But she said that in the future she could see me giving away big things like cars – things they thought they could never afford. She saw me writing people checks. She said I shouldn't be afraid to do that because I would always have more to give.

The young man addressed me again. The dude had gotten giddy and he was bouncing and smiling and giggling. He said he sensed so much Jesus in me. He saw Jesus in my eyes and the way I carried myself. He said, "Wow, this is great!" He started hugging me, and then he rocked back and forth and kept saying wow. He laughed and laughed, and so did I. It was so refreshing, so warm, so powerful. I knew the Lord had done it. That night was a spiritual rebirth.

Driving home, I was ecstatic that I'd reached a new level of interaction with the divine. My skeptical mind had been given new reasons to believe that God is alive.

***

But my ecstasy was short-lived. Something else I soon learned was that whenever I experienced a spiritual high, Satan was almost certain to attack me immediately to throw me off balance.

I went home that night so stoked. I couldn't wait to bring Lydia to that church and to learn for myself how to pray so powerfully. But when I arrived home I found that Lydia had an awful night with the kids. She was sobbing and at her wits' end. Her despondency sucked the excitement right out of me. The spiritual high was gone, overpowered, at least for a while by the darkness that had set up residence in our home. The Devil was using her depression to keep both of us numb to the invigorating, cathartic presence of the Spirit within us. I had no time to tell Lydia my story. We went to bed exhausted. I was drained. But hope remained.

During that season in our life I was working in Nashville for the State of Tennessee, and I rode a commuter bus to work in the mornings. During the 45-minute ride that Monday morning, I prayed for deliverance and healing for my wife. I was struggling to rekindle the fire God lit in me on Sunday night. The bus dropped me off, and I kept praying as I walked up the hill in front of the State Capitol building.

Then something new happened. Something about the quality of my prayer changed. My prayer didn't feel like I was forming the words myself with my own mind. It felt like the words were coming *through* me, originating from an outside source. And these words were strong and powerful and confident and definitive. I heard myself praying forcefully for specific things to happen to specific parts of Lydia's body. When it was over, it felt like something supernatural had washed over me. I had been praying "in the Spirit," just like in the Bible. I never quite understood that phrase before, but now I knew experientially what praying in the Spirit meant. And I felt like I knew Lydia would be healed.

In fact, our life rapidly did improve. My wife and kids all attended the new church over the next several months. One night in worship, I invited the Lord to speak to me. He said, "Ask and it shall be given to you." I told him I had been asking, but why hadn't he healed Lydia? Jesus replied, "I am healing Lydia. I'm making her stronger than you can imagine." Lydia's healing was gradual, but week by week her struggles seemed to soften. There was new hope in our hearts that we were on a trajectory toward healing.

Lydia no longer receives new songs every day, but she does often have vibrant and meaningful dreams. God ushered in healing through the songs, and now he is teaching her in the night with stories and visions and symbols that speak directly to her heart.

The other thing that happened at the new church was that, by simply being able to watch people *using* God's supernatural gifts, I was able to begin using them myself. Although I'm a life-long student of scripture, I'm still just a novice in this new Spirit -filled life. But I knew the scriptures, and I knew that what I encountered in the Spirit-filled church reflected the experience of the churches in the New Testament.

The combination of the new joy we have found together with the realization that God empowers us to do amazing things even today has emboldened my wife and I to help people, to teach the good news, and to promote God's kingdom more effectively than ever before. It made me start my blog and write this book!

It makes me a little sad and angry when I think of all the years I struggled to make a difference in the world unaware of the power that was dormant in me all along. But I trust in God's providence that the years I spent as an academically oriented rule-keeper prepared me to more greatly appreciate the indwelling of the Spirit when its full potential was revealed to me. Lydia has also told me that her six year journey through the vale of depression has equipped her to help depressed people. God keeps putting her in contact with people in despair. And now, Lydia can tell them she knows there is hope because she has survived depression herself. Truly the pain has make us stronger than we could have ever been otherwise.

I am now a more powerful muscle for God than ever. I am more able to respond to the will of the Great Mind because I am more attuned to his living voice. And I have a greater capability for healing broken people and breaking Satan's strongholds because I've learned to tap into the power he offers through the gifts of the Spirit.

***

Heaven's muscle is what I challenge you to become. A muscle does not act to satisfy its own needs; it only serves the brain. It moves when it's told to, it rests when resting is appropriate. But muscles create action, and action generates change. My prayer for you is that you will align your will to the signals from God and allow him to be the intellect that controls your every action.

Muscles must communicate with the brain. They must be attentive to its signals. That's why it's so important to pray – and not just to talk in prayer, but to be quiet and listen. If muscles don't receive the signal, they don't know when to flex, and the world goes on unchanged.

Muscles also grow as they are being used. My prayer for both of us is that we will grow stronger as we flex ourselves in doing good deeds. The more we listen to God's voice and obey it, the stronger we get and the easier it becomes to live a righteous life.

My muscle metaphor is similar to the New Testament vision of living by the life of Christ. Jesus says he did only what the Father told him to. (John 5:19 -20). The minds of Christ and the Father were fused as one. (John 10:3). Paul similarly explained that by the Spirit his own mind was synchronized to the mind of Christ. (Galatians 2:19-20; 1 Corinthians 2:10-16). Spirit-filled Christians cede control of their lives to their Savior. (Romans 6:13-22). Christ fills us, and we follow his lead. (Romans 8:3-14). We can do this because we know his word and listen to his living voice.

And, walking in harmony with God's will as God's earthly muscles, we become capable of doing greater and greater things, just as Jesus promised:

Very truly, I tell you, the one who believes in me will also do the works that I do and, in fact, will do greater works than these, because I am going to the Father. I will do whatever you ask in my name, so that the Father may be glorified in the Son. If in my name you ask me for anything, I will do it. (John 14:12-14).

***

Self-knowledge is the most powerful knowledge next to knowing Christ. I want to open up about myself to facilitate your own self-exploration. I've invested a lot of time in getting to know myself, and I'm not bragging when I discuss my gifts. They're from God, and they come with responsibility attached. Consider praying for God to show you what he's uniquely equipped you to do.

First, God has given me wisdom. When I was a teenager, the words of James 1:5-6 built their own little nest in my noggin, and they've never left:

If any of you is lacking in wisdom, ask God, who gives to all generously and ungrudgingly, and it will be given you. But ask in faith, never doubting.

I prayed daily for many years for God to give me wisdom. It's what this scripture encouraged me to do – pray for wisdom, confident I'd receive it – and wisdom would be mine. I always treasured wisdom and I hope the fruit of my life demonstrates that I've made wise choices.

Second, God has given me the gift of faith.

Sometimes you get prophecies from the most unexpected places. Toward the end of my time as a campus minister, an older gentleman who attended a rather conservative church announced to me one afternoon that he was going to prophecy about me. He made a single proclamation, and it was that God had given me the gift of faith.

At first, this struck me as almost absurd. Intellectually accepting the existence of the supernatural has been very difficult for me. I was an atheist or agnostic for almost three years. My mind programmed to be critical (I'm a lawyer!), and I can always think of reasons to doubt the veracity of my spiritual experiences and even the existence of God. Buying into the popular naturalistic view of the universe is very tempting to me, especially as a person who works among academics.

But recall that the biblical word "faith" does not mean intellectual assent. Faith is a species of action. Biblical faith is faithfulness, or dependability. And I think having faith in God often means being able to act in spite of fear. When that man in Florida said God had given me faith, what he really meant was that God had made me fearless. The man followed up his prophecy with an example. He pointed out that I had dropped everything and left my home in Tennessee to commandeer an oddly-constituted and experimental campus ministry with no real experience in doing that sort of thing. And now, I was about to drop all of that and train for a new career simply because a voice in the night had told me to.

The man was saying I was skilled at making leaps of faith. I pray for this gift for you, that fear will never hold you back.

Third, God has given me the gift of love. This gift was also an unlikely one at the outset. My family is emotionally reserved. You would be forgiven for diagnosing my parents and grandparents as Stoics. Even as a child, I felt that emotions were weaknesses. I longed to achieve full self-mastery. I knew what the Bible said about the tongue being untamable, about the tempting power of the appetite, and about the weaknesses of sinful flesh. I loved how Paul said in First Corinthians 9:27 that he beat his own body to keep it under submission. So I adopted a television character as my personal hero.

It was Mr. Spock from Star Trek. I believed, like Mr. Spock, that people should suppress their emotions and follow pure logic. Mr. Spock was wrong, of course. It failed to dawn on me that the stories on Star Trek were written to expose the limitations of pure logic. Captain Kirk's emotional "hunches" often turned out to be more correct than Mr. Spock's deductions based on empirical evidence. But I thought Mr. Spock was terribly wise, and I wanted to be like him.

But a funny thing happens when you read the Bible a lot. What happened around the time I started college was that I began noticing in the Gospels that Jesus wasn't really like Mr. Spock. Jesus got angry. Jesus could be affectionate. Jesus was sometimes "moved with compassion." The Christ I read about was motivated by love more than by rational calculations. I knew I wanted to be like Jesus. And I knew

I had found a key difference between the mind of Christ and my own mind. I began praying earnestly for God to make me capable of the deep compassionate love that Christ displayed in the Gospels. Just as I had prayed for wisdom as a kid, I now prayed (with trepidation) for a tender heart.

God really delivered. Before long, I could feel my heart swelling every time I was around my friends or people in need. I started loving people so much it literally hurt. I became a hugger. I started having deep, emotionally devastating heart-to-heart talks with people about their griefs and fears, about the abuses they'd suffered, and the lives that had been lost. I became a safe shoulder for people to cry on.

Of all the things I've done in my life, I think I've felt most effectively used by God in those moments when I was quietly bearing the raw emotions of people who were intensely suffering. I am honored and humbled that people have confided in me and let me be their counselor. Just like that dear nursing student said during my first prophetic prayer, I am a beating heart, and God pours love into other people through me. Maybe you should also pray for God to help you love people the way he loves.

On top of the gifts of wisdom & knowledge, faith & fearlessness, and love & compassion, I think God's

given me a gift of communication. But as I said before, that's for you to decide.

Another gift I have is Lydia. I want to thank her for
letting me talk about her so much in this book. She's
awesome. She's my secret weapon.

I pray that God will increase your spiritual gifts, so
you can bear fruit that changes lives. May he show
you what he's designed you to do, so you can take
action.

SIX: ACTION

A slack muscle gets nothing done. And people are designed to find fulfillment in creative and useful work. This holds true for believers and unbelievers alike. Being kind, making art, conquering fears, enjoying nature, and many other creative, loving, and positive things that people do can nurture joy and contentment no matter what your belief system might be. God made us in his image. God himself is a creator and a lover, and when we love and create, we're doing what we were made to do.

One impetus for this book is a sermon I heard at the church in south Nashville. The pastor told the story of an explorer (Hernán Cortés) who recruited people from Cuba to go search for treasure in the new world. After his group arrived in Mexico, the leader gave the order to burn all the ships. Once Cortes's armies reached their destination, there was no turning back. The only way they'd ever make it home again was to find the treasure and use it to build new boats.

Take that leap of faith. Join God's mission. Our job is to continue writing the story of the world God wants to write. God's mission is a mission of healing humanity and healing the earth. God's muscles are fighting against demonic powers. They're exposing the harm that sin inflicts, and calling people to repentance. They're becoming experts at surrendering their egos. God's work, as Second Corinthians chapter six describes it, is the work of reconciliation. It's about getting things back in the order they were meant to be. It's about reversing the curse, and replacing the surface-level meaninglessness of human existence with the nutritious balm of genuine love.

***

Because we are all differently-shaped and differently -equipped muscles, our styles of serving God will necessarily be different. That's how the Maker designed it. God loves diversity and variety! Recall that Romans 12 and First Corinthians 12 discussed the different gifts God gives people, and how the gifts are all critical, even if they don't all appear important on the surface.

The point is to do what you're designed to do. Don't feel bad that you may not be equipped to do what other people are doing. And don't look down on people who are worshiping and serving God in ways that don't resonate with you.

You might think about reading *Sacred Pathways* by Gary Thomas. You may be familiar with *The Five Love Languages*, a book that describes the different ways people express their feelings of love. *Sacred Pathways* does this for worship, and explains how people (and even congregations and denominations) with different personality types find different ways to serve God that resonate with their own spiritual constitutions.

Gary Thomas identifies nine different "pathways." Each "pathway" is a cluster of activities or locations or states of mind that describe how people with different personalities feel close to God. Each "pathway" has its own strengths, and each bears its own dangers. Here's a quick rundown:

- "Naturalists" feel close to God in nature. They feel transported in the mysterious electricity of the forest, in the sounds of chirping birds and scurrying fauna, in the austere majesty of a desert at twilight.

- "Sensates" respond powerfully to beautiful sounds, smells, tastes, pictures, and textures. God can touch their heart through the melody of a song or the power of a painting.

- "Traditionalists" feel connected to their Maker through ritual and symbol. Daily Bible reading and prayer, and faithfulness in attending worship services, are high on their list of priorities.

- "Ascetics" are attracted to solitude and simplicity. They worship best when alone and undistracted. They may be very strict with themselves. Fasting and denying other worldly pleasures helps them feel holy.

- "Activists" feel driven to confront the root causes of suffering in the world. They feel that God's mission for them is to generate social change to heal systemic problems like poverty, disease, and inequality.

- "Caregivers" feel that God's will for them is to comfort and serve individuals. They imitate Christ by loving others on a one-on-one basis.

- "Enthusiasts" are drawn to spiritual highs and experiences of mystery. They love to worship thorough celebrations. They like to create things, and they pray with passion.

- "Contemplatives" have a more mystical approach in that they love to simply adore God. A contemplative feels closest to Christ while meditating and soaking in God's love.

- "Intellectuals" pursue God through study. They want to know as much as possible about him, and they want to be right. They love God with their minds.

My quick list here is very broad and general. And people typically operate in more than one pathway. The important thing is that just as folks have different gifts, folks also have different triggers that help them feel close to God. There's room in the kingdom for traditionalists and sensates, activists and contemplatives, to live together as one diverse body.

And, as Gary Thomas reminds his readers, just because you're not a "caregiver" by nature doesn't mean God doesn't expect you to care for people. You may not be an activist, but God still expects you to strive for justice. You may not be a traditionalist, but you still need to pray, study God's word, and worship with other believers.

As for me, I'm a contemplative naturalist with some intellectual and ascetic tendencies. This combination gives me a set of strengths and weaknesses that probably differs from yours.

God made you who you are, so feel free to be yourself. Your best, holiest self.

***

Perhaps you feel ready to act. Let me tell you more about who's going to be acting through you. Here comes my last story.

We already named and considered many of the malevolent spirits that stain the Bible's pages. While some of these "spirits" may refer to states of mind or tendencies of the structures of human existence, the biblical writers also clearly believed the universe harbored invisible beings whose mission was to spread suffering and death and impede God's work of healing and reconciliation. In addition to the spirits that bodily possessed people (like the Legion), we saw lying spirits, spirits of confusion, spirits of error and false teaching, tormenting spirits, spirits of fatigue, spirits of whoredom, spirits of jealousy, spirits of betrayal, spirits of divination, and even spirits of infirmity that caused physical symptoms.

The other side of this supernatural coin is God's Holy Spirit, the Spirit of Christ, which the Bible also describes in terms of his effects on people. The Holy

Spirit in scripture is his own person with his own story.

The Holy Spirit first appears at the creation of the cosmos. The Spirit is an agent that brings order out of chaos, beauty from cacophony. The Spirit (the word also means wind or breath), is said to hover, blow, or brood over the surface of the primeval waters as the earth is initially formed. (Genesis 1:2). Then, God sculpts the first human from the mud and breathes into this person the breath of life, again invoking the language of spirit, wind, and breath. In fact, a biblical songwriter says that God's creatures are made when he sends his Spirit (Psalm 104:30), and a character in the epic poem of Job says "The Spirit of God has made me" (Job. 33:4). God's Spirit is the carrier of creativity.

Throughout the Hebrew Bible, the Spirit often denotes God's presence on the earth, especially God's presence among his chosen people. (See Genesis 6:3; Psalm 139:7; Isaiah 34:16; 63:10-11; Haggai 2:5). But the Spirit is not only the wind of God that blows incessantly over the earth; the Spirit is also described as water – water God can pour onto or into his people to nourish and strengthen them. (See Isaiah 32:15; 44:3; Ezekiel 36: 25-27; 39:29; Joel 2:28-29; Zechariah 12:10).

The activity of the Spirit certainly does not end with creation. The Spirit is also intimately associated with prophetic activity. For example, after he anoints Saul to be king of Israel, Samuel tells him:

The Spirit of the Lord will come upon you in power, and you will prophecy with [a band of musical prophets]; and you will be changed into a different person. . . . [D]o whatever your hand finds to do, for God is with you. (1 Samuel 10:6-7).

Often in the Bible the "Spirit of the Lord" comes upon a person before he issues a prophetic announcement or begins a career of prophecy. (See 1 Chronicles 12:18; 2 Chronicles 15:1; 20:14; 24:20; Isaiah 48:16; 61:1; Ezekiel 2:2; 3:24; 11:5). And, the Spirit is said to give visions (Ezekiel 11:24) and the interpretation of dreams (Genesis 41:38).

But perhaps just as frequently, the Spirit in the Old Testament is an equipper. The Spirit gives people the courage and the skills to accomplish whatever job God assigns them.

The book of Exodus recounts how the Israelites in the wilderness begin building their extravagant tent of worship, the tabernacle. To facilitate this construction project, the Lord fills a man named Bezalel with "the Spirit of God, with skill, ability, and knowledge in all kinds of crafts" to do the decorative work on the tabernacle. (Exodus 31:3; 35:31). Also in an artistic vein, Exodus 28:3 speaks of people whom God filled with the spirit of wisdom to equip them to design the garments of the priests.

The ancient Jewish book of Sirach (also known as "Ecclesiasticus") isn't in the Bible, but this apocryphal book has a passage that describes the life of the serious Bible student, and explains how the Spirit equips him to study and teach:

He seeks out the wisdom of all the ancients,

and is concerned with prophecies;

he preserves the sayings of the famous

and penetrates the subtleties of parables;

he seeks out the hidden meanings of proverbs

and is at home with the obscurities of parables.

. . . .

If the great Lord is willing,

he will be filled with the spirit of understanding;

he will pour forth words of wisdom of his own

and give thanks to the Lord in prayer.

The Lord will direct his counsel and knowledge,

as he meditates on his mysteries.

He will show the wisdom of what he has learned,

and will glory in the law of the Lord's covenant.

(Sirach 39:1-3, 6-8).

First Chronicles 28:12 says the Spirit installed plans for the temple in David's mind, plans which he then passed on to Solomon. At the end of the Babylonian exile period, Zerubbabel is empowered by the Spirit to rebuild the Jewish temple. (Zechariah 4:6-7). A prophecy also says that God will put his Spirit on the Messiah, which will enable the Messiah to bring "justice to the nations," itself an important creative activity. (Isaiah 42:1).

The Bible describes the Spirit of the Lord as the Spirit of wisdom, understanding, counsel, power, knowledge, and the fear of the Lord. (Isaiah 11:2). We can see the fruit of this supernatural gifting, for example, in Joshua, who "was full of the spirit of wisdom, because Moses had laid his hands on him; and the Israelites obeyed him, doing as the Lord had commanded Moses." (Deuteronomy 34:9).

In the Old Testament, the Spirit also equips people for battle, giving them supranormal courage and sometimes superhuman strength. In Judges, the Spirit of the Lord comes upon Othniel, to make him a warrior judge. (Judges 3:10). The same happens to Gideon, who was timid before the Spirit got him. (Judges 6:34). The same can be said of another military leader named Jephthah. (Judges 11:29). The famous strongman Samson is stirred by the Spirit of the Lord (Judges 13:25), which comes upon him in power (Judges 14:6, 19; 15:14), giving him preternatural brawniness.

Remember when young David fought the giant Goliath? The Bible tells us that the Spirit of the Lord had already come upon him "with power" when Samuel previously anointed him. (1 Samuel 16:13).

Also notice what God says to the Jewish exiles in Ezekiel 36:24-27. Here, we have the Spirit associated with water and cleansing, and the Spirit enables the people to finally be obedient to God's laws:

I will take you out of the nations; I will gather you from all the countries and bring you back into your own land. I will sprinkle clean water on you, and you will be clean; I will cleanse you from all your impurities and from all your idols. I will give you a new heart and put a new spirit in you; I will remove from you your heart of stone and give you a heart of flesh. And I will put my Spirit in you and move you to follow my decrees and be careful to keep my laws.

We see this passage fulfilled in Romans 8, where Christians now walk under the direction of the Spirit, and "the just requirement of the law" is fulfilled in them. In other words, the presence of God's Spirit enables people to be fully obedient.

Another passage that prophetically describes the time surrounding the coming of Christ is Zechariah 12:10, which says, "I will pour out a *spirit of compassion and supplication* on the house of David and the inhabitants of Jerusalem, so that, when they look on the one whom they have pierced, they shall mourn for him, as one mourns for an only child, and weep bitterly over him, as one weeps over a firstborn."

This wisdom and courage and compassion and creativity that the Spirit dispenses on God's people also brings a sense of liberation and transformation. Second Corinthians 3:16-18 says that when a person turns to the Lord, the veil that restrains their understanding is removed:

Now the Lord is the Spirit, and where the Spirit of the Lord is, there is freedom. And all of us, with unveiled faces, seeing the glory of the Lord as though reflected in a mirror, are being transformed into the same image from one degree of glory to another; for this comes from the Lord, the Spirit.

And that brings us back to my battle-cry from Chapter Zero: "God did not give us a spirit of cowardice, but rather a spirit of power and of love and of self-discipline." (2 Timothy 1:7). The prophet Micah captures this spirit of moral courage perhaps even more clearly in Micah 3:6-8. After predicting disgrace for the false prophets, Micah proclaims:

But as for me, I am filled with power,

with the spirit of the Lord,

and with justice and might,

to declare to Jacob his transgression

and to Israel his sin.

This sort of courage is what God wants to give you. Nothing kills faith quite like fear. So much good goes undone in the world because God's children are afraid to step outside their zones of comfort. I'm asking you as a muscle to offer yourself wholly to God, and then have the courage to do whatever he calls and equips you to do. Do it with power. Do it with "justice and might." Even if it's something difficult, like shining a light on sin, inequality, or bad religion.

So we've considered the things the Spirit has done – and keeps doing – throughout history. The Spirit is creativity. The Spirit coaxes order and beauty out of chaos. The Spirit breathes life into things that are lifeless. Although the Spirit is as unpredictable and mysterious as the wind, the Spirit is also a fountain of wisdom and revelation. The Spirit carries knowledge. And the Spirit can make people stronger and more courageous than they'd ever be on their own. The Spirit can make you a new person. The Spirit helps you walk in the Lord's will. The Spirit can equip you for battle and plant plans in your mind and words in your mouth. Do not underestimate what you have been given.

***

At the heart of all of this, of course, is the sacrificial love of Jesus Christ. Christ's obedience and atoning sacrifice broke the back of Satan's stronghold and set mankind free from frustration and meaninglessness.

And God's goal – the engine that drives the biblical story – is reconciliation. God created humans because he loves to love and be loved. When we join his mission, we join his work of healing souls, of restoring relationships. We bring people together while also leading them toward God. Our work is the work of loving people because loving is what God does.

***

The theme of this chapter has been action. I invite you now to think of actions you can take to more fully seize your freedom in Christ, to draw closer to him, to activate your inner gifts, and to allow the Lord's indwelling presence to guide your life. What prayers do you need to pray? What Bible passages do you feel drawn to revisit? Is there anyone you could talk to who could help you explore your gifts and your opportunities to serve the Lord? Are there habits you need to give up? Temptations you need to conquer? Lies you need to rebuke? Spirits you need to drive out? Are you attached to a church that's more stifling than liberating?

I give you permission and freedom to question and explore. It's okay to leap out in faith. It's okay to get lost in the mystery of God, to give up easy answers and formulas. It's okay to doubt, because that's really just a form of humility. If your heart is drawn to the heart of Jesus, then you're in good hands. I encourage you to unhook your spiritual training wheels. You can choose the unpredictable life, the life controlled by the indwelling Christ. It's better than man's packaged religious systems and dogmas. Just be sure to pray for wisdom and truth, keep scripture as your anchor, and stay connected to mature believers you can trust.

***

I recently moved to a town in eastern Kentucky. It was hard leaving the church we'd discovered a year before, where the Spirit seemed so active and palpable. But God has provided. The first church we visited in our new hometown turned out to be a wonderful Spirit-filled family of creative lovers of Jesus. We were immediately at home. And God does cool and weird stuff there.

A couple of weeks ago, during a Wednesday night service, the pastor preached about Christians' authority over the evil powers. At the end, he asked everyone who wanted to seize that authority to assemble at the front of the auditorium. As he prayed for the people one by one, each person collapsed onto the ground. It was like something on TV, the kind of thing I used to scoff at. I'd never seen such a thing in person, and had never expected to. What would happen when he came and prayed over me?

But on that night in July 2014, I remembered that God is interested in every aspect of ourselves – body, mind, soul, and spirit. All are connected. What happens in our minds or our spirits can affect our bodies, and vice-versa. The positions in which we pray or praise can affect the way we interact with God. And scripture shows that falling down is a natural response to the presence of the divine. (Mark 3:11; Luke 5:8, 8:28; Revelation 5:14, 19:4, 22:8).

So, part of me was skeptical. But I was eager to receive whatever blessing God might give. And I was especially eager to honor whatever the Lord was doing in that church. I approached the pastor with a willing heart, vowing inside myself to go wherever God wanted to take me. I doubted I'd collapse on the floor, though.

The pastor took my hands. First, he told me a little prophetic stuff about myself that I had already sensed was true. Then he told me to relax and to invite the Spirit into my heart. I mentally placed myself in God's hands and tried to breathe the Spirit into my lungs. There was a moment of absolute quiet. Then the pastor simply flicked his wrists, said one sentence, and I went tumbling to the floor.

I tumbled to the floor like a collapsing Jenga puzzle. I never would have expected that to happen to me. But weird stuff can happen when you let God take the reigns. Of course, I couldn't even fall down in the Spirit correctly. The pastor and I were standing next to the stage, and when my legs gave out under me, my knees slammed into the stage with a loud smack. Everybody stopped what they were doing to check if I was okay. I felt fine. No bruises, no problem.

In fact, I felt great. I felt like the line the pastor told me was true. When he flicked his wrist and sent me careening to the floor, he said, "You're set free." Those words echoed in my head as I sat there in the dim warmth of the church sanctuary, quietly giggling, a smile plastered across my face. God was good. I'd been set free. Where the Spirit of the Lord is, there is freedom.

Less than a week later, I was writing this book. I'm trying to pass on this gift of freedom to you, if it isn't yours already. Jesus and I want you to be set free. I've been set free from the spirit of timidity. I've been set free from bad religion. I'm free to answer God's call with my whole heart, and I know he'll continue to enlighten and empower me as my Lord and I explore and discover the future together.

Let Jesus take your hand. Smile at him and walk with confidence and joy wherever he wants to lead you.

You're set free.

You're set free.

You're set free.

AFTERWORD

Thank you for joining me through this humble book. There is much more to say about Jesus, about scripture, about the church. I hope we can continue this conversation in the future. Perhaps you found yourself saying, "I wish he'd explain that concept in more detail," or, "I wished he'd give more scriptures to support that idea." We can totally have that conversation.

You can get in touch through my website. It's at:

www.BrenHughes.com

I encourage you to subscribe to my mailing list there. If you liked this book, please consider writing a short review on Amazon.com. And order a copy for a friend.

But most importantly, I encourage you to act on the ideas we've explored. How can you take what we've

learned about spiritual warfare, freedom from bad
religion, and the empowerment of the indwelling
Spirit and apply them in ways that help you fulfill
the Lord's threefold requirement that you "do justice," "love kindness," and "walk humbly with your
God?" (Micah 6:8). How can you be heaven's muscle right now? Who do you know who needs a little
heaven in their life today? What gifts do you want
to ask God to give you? Have you assessed the gifts
you already have? Do you need to commit your life
to following Jesus? Do you need to be baptized? To
find a church where God lives and breathes? Please
don't put this book down until you've made a deci-
sion to act in some way that brings you closer to the
Lord.

***

Think back to that night in Panama I described in
chapter zero. As I sat on that mountain, while my
brain denied the existence of God, something deeper
within me knew that I was not alone. That I had a
mission. And that I was loved. God's Spirit desired
me so strongly, he pursued me and drew me back
onto the path of being a spiritual teacher. He desires
you, too. And there's something in the world that
needs to be done that only you can do. Through the
medium of this book, our minds have met at this very

moment so that a spark might suddenly sizzle inside you. So that God can flip on the lightswitch that lets you see what's inside yourself that you've been missing. No matter how old you are, in Christ the adventure is always just beginning.

If you are captive to negative thoughts, to lies, or to bad religion, I proclaim freedom to you. Christ has done what's necessary to set you free from such things. Know that you are loved, that you are safe in him, that you are forgiven. You live by grace; you are not under law. You're set free. This is the year of the Lord's favor. Through us, his earthly muscles, God is bringing justice into the world.

By the time *Heaven's Muscle* hits the presses, I should already be working on my next book. It's called *My Body is a Weapon*. It's a book about masculinity. I'm writing it to challenge men to renounce the sexual stereotypes the world tries to foist on us. I'm going to challenge my fellow males to use their God-given creative energies to strive for justice in specific ways. We'll explore concepts like physicality, emotions, friendship, sexuality, romance, careers, power and powerlessness, identity, anger, gender, and privilege. Please pray as I write that the Lord will use my keystrokes as a tool to free men's minds and enlarge their hearts. May Jesus use me to help make this world more like heaven.

Acknowledgments

While I've still got you here, I want to give some shout-outs to some people who have helped me on my spiritual journey.

This book is dedicated to my wife. Our striving and suffering together has made our spirits hard as steel.

I also honor some other individuals who have ministered with me, ministered to me, or challenged me to think new thoughts. Not all of them would agree with this book's contents, but I love them all and want to give honor where it is due:

- Howard & Anna Vosburgh

- Jon & Rachel Eppley

- John Mark Hicks (JohnMarkHicks.com)

- Caleb McMillen

- Clint & Jodi Thomas (SlowBurnNashville.com)

- Scott Wright & fam. (VineyardofLondon.com)

- Daniel & Rachel Gordon

- The late Dowell Flatt

- Ralph Gilmore

- Owen D. Olbricht

- Frank Viola (FrankViola.org)

- Rhea Perry (EducatingForSuccess.com)

- Brian & Tulisha Scott

I also want to thank those who have helped me in the preparation and promotion of this book:

- Justin Hammonds (JustinHammonds.com)

- Tammy Belcher

- Keith & Jennifer Heyboer

- Jared & Heather Throneberry

- Rita Woods Aaron

- Mary O'Neil

The drawings on the cover come from the *Anatomy of Humane Bodies* (1698), published by William Cowper (1666-1709).

And perhaps most importantly, I thank you for reading this humble book and sharing it with your friends. God bless you all.

About the Author

Bren Hughes is an attorney and native of Nashville, Tennessee. He's currently on a temporary government assignment in eastern Kentucky, where he lives with his wife and three sons. A former minister, Bren holds a B.A. in biblical studies and an M.A. in biblical languages from Freed-Hardeman University. He also holds an M.Div. from Lipscomb University's Hazelip School of Theology and a Juris Doctorate from Vanderbilt University Law School. Bren's *Heaven's Muscle* blog has encouraged people around the world. This is his first book.

BIBLE CREDITS